CRISES • BAILOUTS • INSTABILITY
There is a path out.
This book will show you the way.

Three men with three different areas of expertise…

R. Nelson Nash made a career in the life insurance industry—where he discovered IBC.

....

L. Carlos Lara has spent decades counseling business owners in financial distress.

....

Robert P. Murphy is a PHD economist with experience in academia and the financial sector.

…All share a passion for the *"Austrian School"* of economics and, in this book, come together to provide business owners and households with a solution to their economic problem: the *Infinite Banking Concept (IBC)*, which allows you to—
"become your own banker."

THE
CASE for IBC

THE
CASE for IBC

How to Secede from Our Current Monetary Regime
One Household at a Time

Second Edition

L. Carlos Lara
Robert P. Murphy, Ph.D.
R. Nelson Nash

Copyright © 2018
By: L. Carlos Lara, Robert P. Murphy and R. Nelson Nash
First Edition-Printed February 2018 in the United States by Sheridan Books, Inc.,
Ann Arbor, Michigan
ISBN 978-0-9997786-0-9

Second Edition-Printed October 2018 in the United States by Sheridan Books, Inc.,
Ann Arbor, Michigan
ISBN 978-0-9997786-1-6

Cover Art and Design by Stephanie Long

Acknowledgements

Everything in this book has been, directly or indirectly, built upon the foundation laid by earlier thinkers. All of the authors are adherents to the Austrian School of economics, and so we thank those who have devoted their lives to the dissemination of these crucial ideas of economic liberty. Nelson Nash would like to single out his debt to Leonard Read in particular, who was Nelson's personal mentor on these matters.

Although he is not listed as a formal co-author, we would like to thank David Stearns, president of Infinite Banking Concepts LLC and director of the Nelson Nash Institute, for his invaluable assistance in developing the content both of this book and, more generally, the IBC Seminar for the general public that was this book's genesis.

Over the years, we have received invaluable assistance from actuaries and the management of mutual life insurance home offices, helping us to better understand the mechanics of Whole Life policies and the operation of these special business structures.

We also salute the graduates of our Authorized IBC Practitioner Program. These financial professionals are "in the trenches" every day, helping business owners and households secede one at a time from the prevailing banking and Wall Street nexus.

As usual, graphic artist Stephanie Long provided the compelling cover image.

Finally, we would like to especially thank Anne Lara, who was instrumental in the preparation of the final manuscript. Anne went above and beyond the call of duty by sacrificing the bulk of her Christmas break to ensuring that the turnaround from Word documents to finished product was achieved in record time.

REPRESENTATIONS:

STATUS: The Authors of this book warrant and represent that they are not "brokers" or to be deemed as "broker-dealers," as such terms are defined in the Securities Act of 1933, as amended, or an "insurance company," or "bank."

LEGAL, TAX, ACCOUNTING, OR INVESTMENT ADVICE: The Authors of this book are not rendering legal, tax, accounting, or investment advice. All exhibits in this book are solely for illustration purposes, but under no circumstances shall the reader construe these as the rendering of legal, tax, accounting or investment advice.

DISCLAIMER AND LIMITATION OF LIABILITY: The Authors of this book hereby disclaim any and all warranties, express, or implied, including merchantability or fitness for a particular purpose and make no representation or warranty of the certainty that any particular result will be achieved. In no event will the Authors, their employees, or associated persons, or agents be liable to the reader of this book, or its Agents for any causes of action of any kind whether or not the reader has been advised of the possibility of such damage.

This book is dedicated to
all those who
love *Liberty* and champion *Sound Money*.

THE
CASE for IBC

How to Secede from Our Current Monetary Regime
One Household at a Time

CONTENTS

Introduction xiii

Chapter 1: Thinking Like a Business Owner 1

Chapter 2: The "Perfect Investment" 15

Chapter 3: Banking and Life Insurance: Process vs. Platform 25

Chapter 4: Becoming Your Own Banker 41

Chapter 5: How Does This Work?
The Economics of IBC 73

Chapter 6: Lessons From History 97

Chapter 7: Putting IBC into Action 107

Appendices 125

About the Nelson Nash Institute 127

About the IBC Practitioner Program 129

Find a Practitioner Near You 131

About the Authors 133

Introduction

This book is a distillation of the IBC Seminar for the general public that was originally conducted by R. Nelson Nash, L. Carlos Lara, and Robert P. Murphy. (Beginning in 2018, the IBC Seminar will be presented by Lara and Murphy.) Although each of us had published books and articles for the public, we realized that we had developed material for live audiences in our seminar that was nowhere in print. This book fills that gap.

The content of the following chapters, as well as the material in the appendices, provides a great deal of information regarding our diverse backgrounds and how we all came together, united in our passion for Austrian economics and "privatized banking." Even so, this Introduction will provide some additional historical context that should hopefully make it easier for the reader to absorb our message.

R. Nelson Nash discovered the Infinite Banking Concept (IBC) in the midst of an epiphany in the early 1980s. Simply put, IBC is a way to use properly designed Whole Life insurance policies to put the banking function back at the "you and me level." By recapturing interest payments that otherwise would flow to outsiders, IBC gives financial independence to business owners and households.

Nash had a successful career in the life insurance business, using his revolutionary insights to help people see banking as a process, rather than as something that "bankers" did. Nash eventually began putting on seminars for the public (around 1996), in order to increase the rate at which he spread his message. Out of these seminars Nash developed the material that became his underground classic, *Becoming Your Own Banker*, which was first published in October 2000. As of this writing, *Becoming Your Own Banker* has sold some 400,000 copies. It is still *the* essential text for anyone wishing to understand IBC.

David Stearns joined Infinite Banking Concepts in June 2004 after retiring from the U.S. Army as a Lieutenant Colonel. Stearns worked closely with Nash to launch the IBC "Think Tank" in August 2005, out of Birmingham, Alabama. The IBC Think Tank is a forum of instruction and fellowship, allowing IBC practitioners to encourage and learn from each other. (Currently the Think Tank is reserved for Authorized IBC Practitioners and their invited guests.)

L. Carlos Lara is a business consultant living in Nashville. Following a personal financial upheaval in the 1980s, he had been led to the Austrian School of economics, and in particular its explanation of the boom-bust cycle. In 2007, while working on a lecture teaching the dangers of fractional reserve banking that he was going to present to commercial bankers (!), Lara consulted a Study Guide on Austrian economics. He discovered that the author, Robert P. Murphy, also lived in Nashville (at the time). Soon after that meeting, it was Lara who introduced Murphy to Nash's book, *Becoming Your Own Banker*. Murphy was intrigued, and after some study, he realized that IBC made perfect sense.

Especially in the wake of the financial crisis and the various rounds of "Quantitative Easing" (QE), Murphy and other academic Austrian economists were warning the public about the dangers of runaway monetary policy. However, the academic Austrians, though experts at diagnosing *the problem* of government interference in our monetary and banking systems, provided no immediate *solution* except to acquire "inflation hedges" such as the precious metals. The long-term solution of course was education and turning public opinion, but this seemed like a very distant goal.

Amidst this pessimism, Lara explained to Murphy that IBC offered a way to achieve "privatized banking" one household or business at a time! Rather than trying to reform the whole system with top-down change, a strategy of *seceding* from the dominant banking/Wall Street nexus was much more effective and peaceful. In order to drive home this message, Lara and Murphy co-authored the book *How Privatized Banking **Really** Works* in 2010.

Lara and Murphy began giving presentations explaining the virtues of IBC to the general public. However, they soon realized a glaring problem: If their writings and public talks convinced members of the public to get an IBC policy, where did these people *go* to get one? Lara and Murphy did not want to actually sell life insurance to the general public, yet a trained financial professional was necessary to make IBC work.

To alleviate this and other concerns, the four men—Nelson Nash, David Stearns, Carlos Lara, and Robert Murphy—established the Infinite Banking Institute (IBI) and the IBC Practitioner's Program, formally launching both at the February 2013 Think Tank. It was later decided that both to solidify his legacy and also to distinguish the organization from copy-cats, the IBI was renamed the Nelson Nash Institute (NNI) at the February 2015 Think Tank.

To this day, these men strive to teach the public—through books, seminars, articles, and podcasts—sound economics in the tradition of the Austrian School, and how to "become your own banker" through the practice of IBC. Further information on the NNI and its operations are available in the Appendices to this book.

The material in this book is necessarily based on the U.S. experience, since that's our area of expertise. However, the growing body of Authorized IBC Practitioners include financial professionals not just from the United States (and its territories) but also Canada. Even so, foreign readers should be aware that the specific Whole Life policy needed for IBC is not currently available in much of the world.

In closing, we offer a warning: The material in this book flies in the face of conventional financial thinking. Yet we can surely agree that conventional financial thinking has put this country in a huge mess. It is high time to take the banking function away from "the experts" and return it to the nation's business owners and households.

Chapter 1

Thinking Like a Business Owner

In our experience, *business owners* tend to see the advantages of the Infinite Banking Concept (IBC) before most other people. This isn't because business owners are smarter or even wealthier than others; indeed there are plenty of very smart and highly paid academics and professionals out there.

The reason business owners "get" IBC right away is that they appreciate the importance of *cash flow*. This is especially true if we have in mind the owner of a relatively large business, with at least several employees and a significant amount of other recurring expenses. A business owner of this kind realizes how it's possible that you could be "doing great this quarter!" while you're also worried about making payroll next week. This apparent contradiction—which actually *isn't* a contradiction—is something that salaried employees won't understand. But anyone who has started a new business or who operates a business enterprise recognizes this mindset perfectly, and in fact could probably share a few funny stories about it.

One of us (Carlos Lara) has spent decades making a career out of consulting with business owners, and often business owners who are in financial distress. (See our official bios at the end of the book for more details.) Because business owners can *see* the virtues of IBC more quickly than most others, this is how we choose to begin our presentation in this book. We will first depict the financial problem of the typical business owner, and then (in the following chapters) you will see how IBC solves the problem.

However, if you aren't a business owner, don't worry. The substance of our diagnosis of the problem, as well as the "cure" we prescribe, all pertain to a *household* too. After all, your household is a financial entity or a "business" broadly construed. (Some months you might feel it is more accurately described as a non-profit!) Yet we have found that members of the public can often grasp the principles of IBC more readily when they look at our current monetary and banking systems with the eyes of a business owner.

To be sure, every person is a unique individual. But there are traits that tend to be shared by business owners, so at the risk of overgeneralizing, in the rest of this chapter we will talk about how "the business owner" thinks and operates. We have in mind the owner of a "small business," which the government officially defines as a firm with fewer than 500 employees. These "small business owners" represent 99.7% of all firms that have employees, and account for roughly half of the total employment in the United States[i]—so the word "small" can be misleading. Indeed, some of these operations are quite extensive.

As we'll see, the typical business owner faces a stacked deck in our current financial landscape. Fortunately, *there is a way to opt out of this rigged game.*

Setting Up the Timeline

The business owner tends to avoid traditional financial products such as stocks and mutual funds. He likes assets, of course, but prefers them to be tangible, *hard* assets—things like buildings, land, and of course *cash*.

The reason business owners shy away from traditional asset classes is that they believe the highest rate of return comes from reinvesting in their business.

The business owner thinks in terms of a 12-month cycle. Mentally, he organizes his business activities annually. (Most small business owners match their business's 12-month cycle to the calendar year.) Of course, the underlying "real" activity is a nonstop flow, but people need a method of classification and so they typically place their events on a timeline running from January to December.

Thinking Like a Business Owner

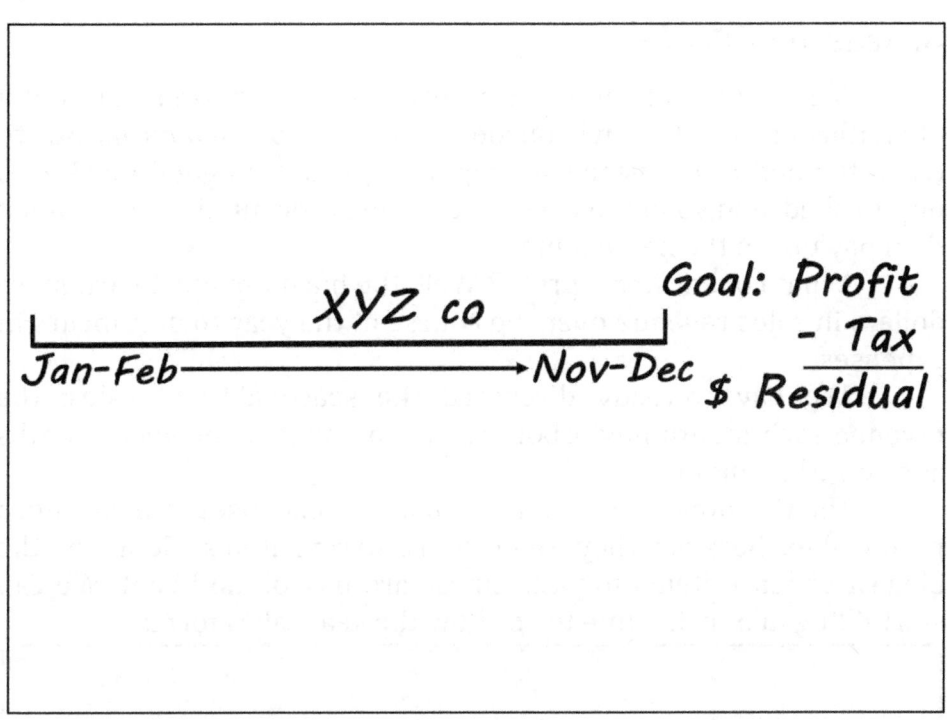

There is a very legitimate reason for organizing a business according to a 12-month cycle: Business sales tend to be *seasonal*. This is obvious for outfits that manufacture or sell fashion footwear and apparel, operate a nursery of landscaping shrubs and trees, or provide tax preparation services, but businesses in general have seasonal sales that repeat on an annual cycle. Consider: Some businesses do 65% of their total sales in the last two months of the year! It would be very misleading to calculate profit & loss statements for such an enterprise in a way that didn't account for the wild swings in revenue that predictably occur every year.

In Search of Profit

Some organizations are explicitly organized to fulfill philanthropic or other civic purposes. But the goal of *a business* is to reach the end of the year showing a *profit*. But no good deed goes unpunished, and so in the event of a business profit, the owner must then pay tax on the net income:

What constitutes a profit? Well, the business must earn more dollars in sales revenue over the course of the year than it incurs in expenses.

We have already discussed the seasonality of sales: the revenue each month might bounce around, with some good months and some bad months.

On the other hand, many business expenses can be more predictable, because they refer to recurring items. Some of the biggest expense items for a business are payroll and rent. We can start filling in our timeline to see how the year takes form:

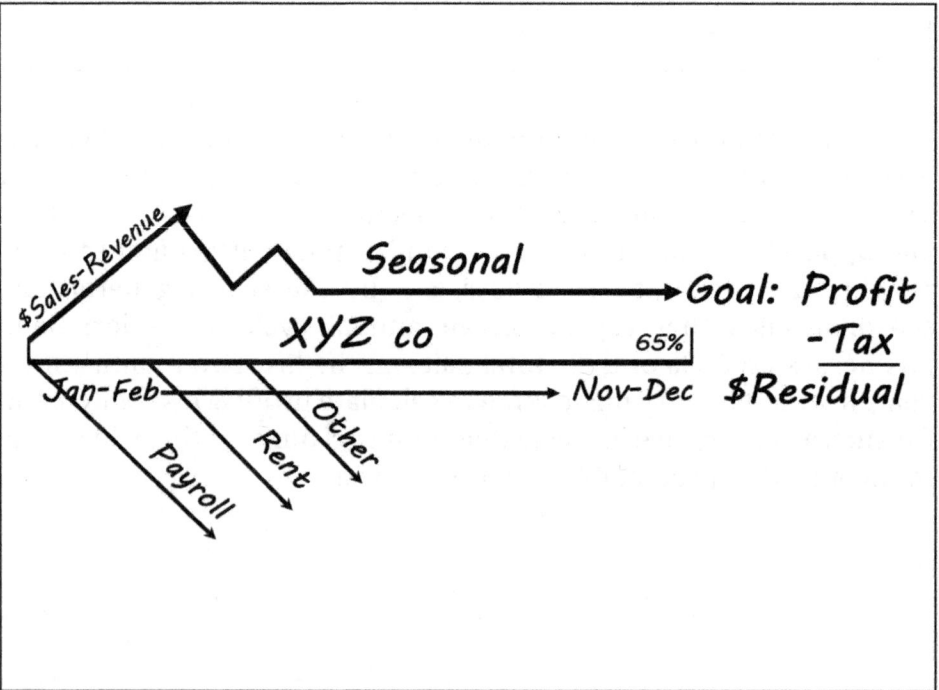

Thinking Like a Business Owner

So far we've been presenting matters as if the business operated purely on a "cash" basis. But as we stressed in the beginning of the chapter, the business owner recognizes the difference between *cashflow* and income. We incorporate the complication of *credit* next.

Show Me the Money: The Role of Credit

Question: How can a business make a sale and yet not have any money to show for it? Answer: When the sale is made *on credit*. That is, for a trusted customer, the business will ship goods (or provide services) in exchange for an IOU (either literally signed or simply assumed in good faith) given by the customer. Such activity is still a sale, and the business has generated income during the period in question, but the actual asset it obtains isn't cash but rather the debt that is now classified under "Accounts Receivable," sometimes abbreviated "A/R."

What this means is that the business owner can enter a new year in January, carrying debts (i.e. Accounts Receivable) from sales that were consummated in the previous calendar year. The accountants can tell the business owner how *late* these debts are. Some may be 30, 60, or even 90 days past due. Rather than continuing to send notices by mail or email, the business owner may decide to get on the phone and *call* the customer in question.

This can often be an amusing experience, as any business owner will attest. The late customer may suddenly volunteer a weather report: "Yes Mr. Green, I've been getting your letters. Gosh you wouldn't be*lieve* it, we got dumped on with a foot of snow! The whole city's shut down. But I'll get that check to you as soon as the roads are clear, I've got it right in my hands."

On the other hand, the business owner himself can *receive* merchandise on credit, taking possession of the goods before actually paying for them. This is handled under "Accounts Payable," sometimes abbreviated "A/P."

Thinking Like a Business Owner

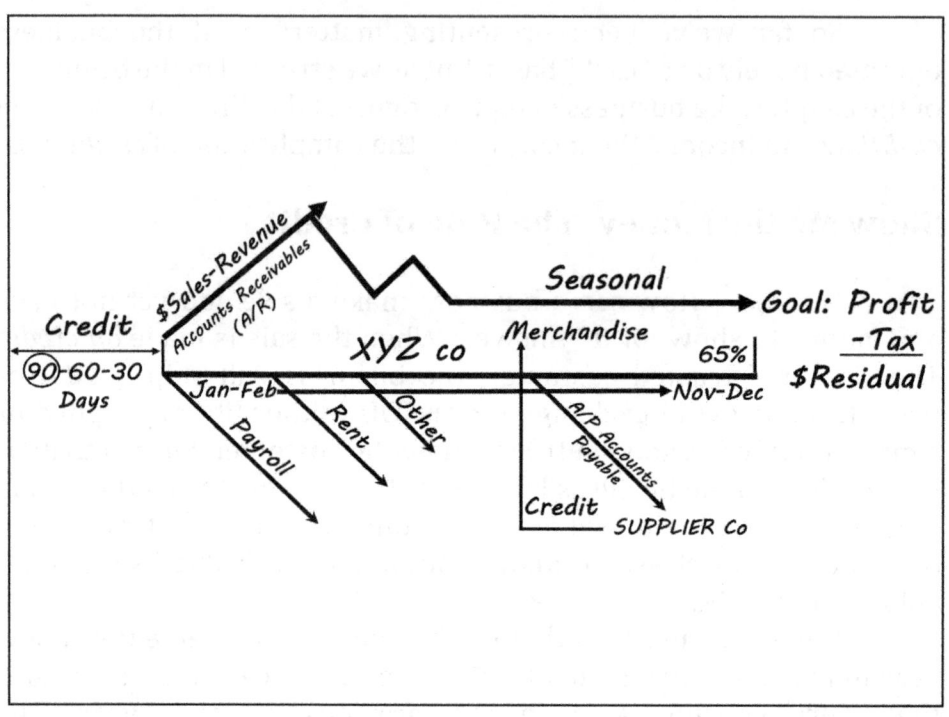

Under normal circumstances, the business owner would receive merchandise on credit, having (say) 30 days to send the check to the supplier. If all goes well, the business owner himself turns the product over (after charging a mark-up) and then can easily afford to pay his bill, reducing the amount in his "Accounts Payable."

At this point, let us stress that *legally speaking*, when a supplier ships merchandise on credit to the business owner, the *title to possession changes hands* when the product hits the shipping dock. At that moment, the business owner is the legal owner of the merchandise, and merely has a *debt* owed to the supplier. We will see soon enough why this fact is so important.

Commercial Banks and Lines of Credit (LOCs)

Consider our diagram at this point. Every month, the business owner has expenses (some of them fixed) that must be paid and yet—as we stressed—the revenues come in sporadically. Even if the business owner ends up with a profit at the *end* of the year, it's entirely possible that he has a cashflow deficit in some months along the way.

Because of this threat, most business owners find it very convenient to open up large lines of credit (LOCs) with one or more commercial banks. Under this arrangement, if the business owner is short in a particular month, the commercial bank steps in to advance the cash needed to keep things running.

If all goes according to plan, the business owner pays down the line of credit soon enough, and everybody is happy. It's similar to paying off his debts owed to the suppliers, if they have advanced him merchandise.

The Commercial Bank's Stranglehold

The problem, of course, comes in when things *don't* go according to plan. If the business owner falls behind in paying off his line of credit, the "friendly neighborhood banker" might have a sudden change in disposition. The business owner's case might get kicked into a different department of the bank.

At first the bank might give him some breathing room by converting the line of credit into a "note," in which the outstanding debt starts rolling over at interest and requires a fixed amount of repayment each month in order to knock it out in a definite amount of time.

Of course, since our business owner is only *in* this position because his business is not going well, it's entirely possible that he starts falling behind in payments on the note.

At this point, the bank may decide to play its hand. We see exactly who is running the show. It turns out that in order to open up that "convenient" line of credit, the business owner first agreed to make his deposits into the commercial bank. But now with regards to notes, he has contractually agreed that the commercial bank would have liens against his business assets, including any machinery, inventory, or even the land itself. Furthermore, bank notes as a general rule require a "personal guarantee" meaning that his personal assets are on the hook too, so that any labor income he earns from other sources may be garnished.

In sum, all of the business owner's "factors of production"—land, labor, and capital—are actually controlled by the commercial bank, including his bank deposits. If he ends up in bankruptcy court, the business owner will find that the bank has "first dibs" on all of his assets.

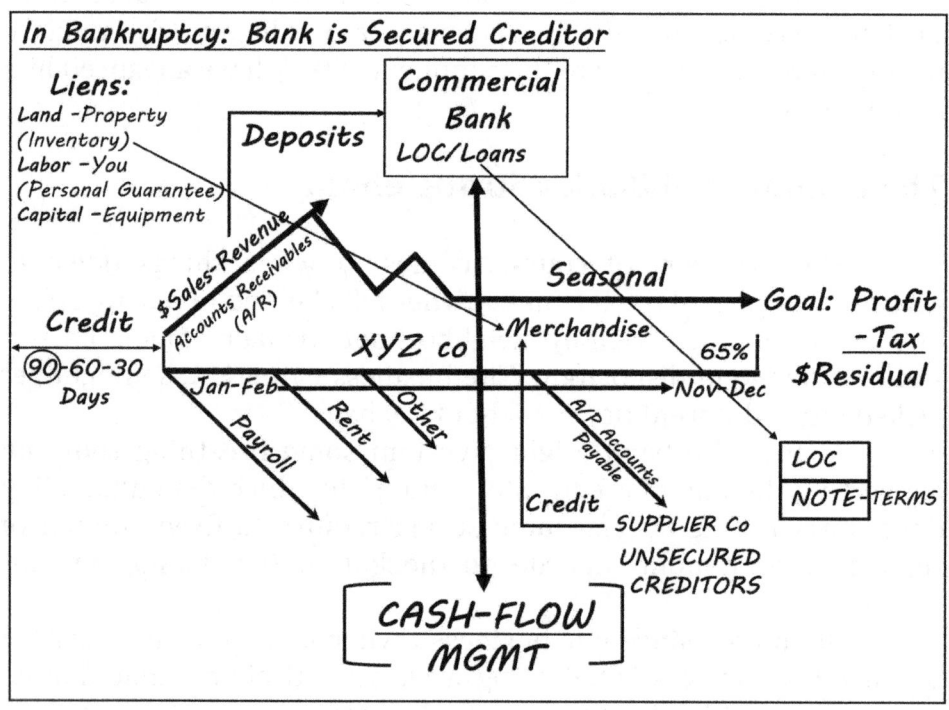

Now what is important to realize is that in the case of a bankruptcy, the *suppliers* of the business owner—the ones who advanced merchandise and whose debt was included under "Accounts Payable"—are also in trouble. For example, suppose the business owner owes the commercial bank $500,000, owes his suppliers $1 million, and yet after the firesale of his assets, only has $700,000 in cash that he can quickly raise. In this case, the commercial bank gets paid off *in full*—all $500,000 of his debt is paid off. Then the remaining $200,000 is used to (partially) pay the suppliers, which is only 20 cents on the dollar.

What has happened in such a scenario is that the commercial bank is the *secured* creditor, meaning it has first right to any business assets. The suppliers are only *unsecured* creditors. They are legally entitled to any residual wealth in the company, to be sure, but if the business goes under, there might not be enough left to go satisfy all of the claims.

Setting Up An "Alternate Bank"

As the above discussion indicates, the typical business owner is in a very precarious position if he relies on commercial bank lines of credit for his cashflow needs. In order to gradually minimize and ultimately eliminate this vulnerability, the business owner should set up an *alternate bank* that provides similar services.

In the remainder of this book, we will show you the details and justify our claims. But at this point, suspend your disbelief and suppose the following is possible:

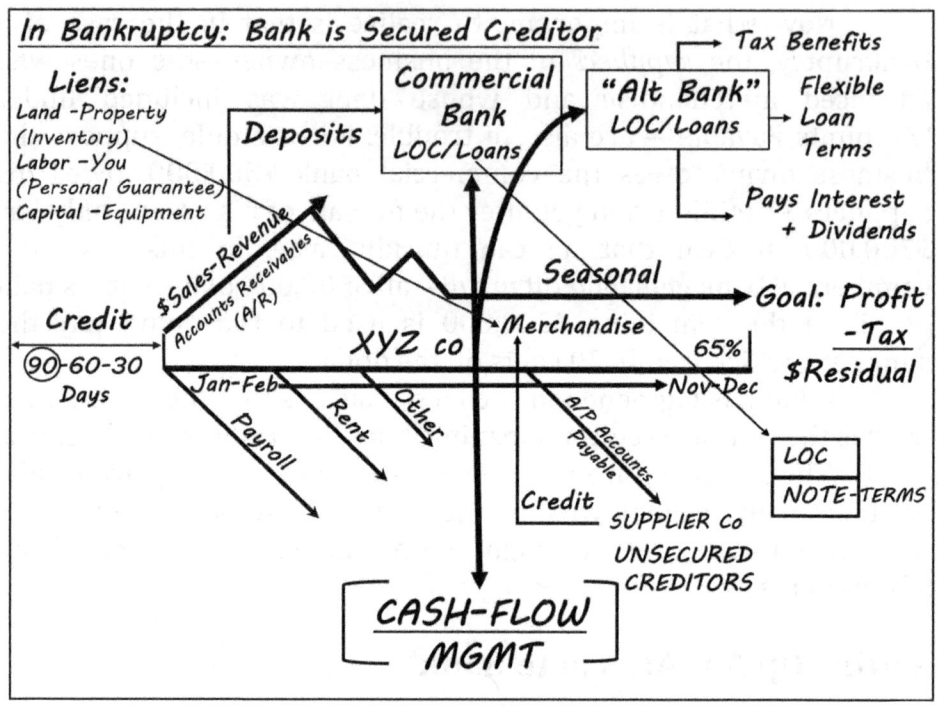

Imagine if there were an "alternate bank" that would also grant "lines of credit" or loans, in order to smooth out the cashflow irregularities of the business, but where there would be no lien on the business assets. Further, this alternate bank would provide much more attractive tax benefits and a better return on the money left inside it. Finally, this alternate bank wouldn't have any particular payback schedule for the loans the business owner took out. In fact, the business owner wouldn't *ever* need to pay back a dime on the loans, if he didn't want to. No one from this alternate bank would come knocking on his door, demanding payment.

We realize this may sound like wishful thinking, but you will see in the coming chapters that we are not joking. For now, we hope you agree that *if* there existed such an "alternate bank," then every business owner would scramble to begin building it up. During good times, before any crisis hits in which the commercial bank's stranglehold would become apparent, the business owner would start "sweeping" any excess money out of the conventional places and into the "alternate bank."

Over time, the larger the alternate bank grew, the less dependent the business owner would be on the traditional financing outlets. The business owner would gradually wean himself from dependence on commercial banks for his cashflow management. He would gradually *secede* from the traditional financial network that has ensnared most Americans.

"But isn't my money at least *safe* in a regular bank?"

In our experience, the chief reason that business owners want to "do their banking" with a conventional commercial bank is that their funds are *safe* there. After all, we have an expression: "money in the bank."

Ah, but things are not as secure as you might believe. In the first place, *legally speaking*, when you deposit funds into a commercial bank, *you are no longer the owner of that money*. On the contrary, you are now a *creditor* of the bank. This goes back centuries to the legal treatment established in England, and carried over to the American colonies.

In other words, when you pull up to the bank in your vehicle and sign over some checks, depositing them in that tube—*whoosh!*—you are actually relinquishing legal ownership of your funds. The bank *owes* you the money, obviously. But legally speaking, you are now a creditor of the bank, and more specifically you are an *unsecured* creditor.

That's right: With respect to your commercial bank, you are in the same vulnerable position as the unsecured creditors of our earlier discussion, who had advanced merchandise but would only get pennies on the dollar in case of a bankruptcy.

This is not fearmongering on our part. After the bank "bail-outs" of 2008, the American public was fed up. The Dodd-Frank Act (signed into law in 2010) was written in "lawyer language" but if you can read it, it clearly spells out that during any *future* crisis, *no more taxpayer money will be used to patch up bank deficiencies.* Instead there will be a "bail-in," meaning that the shareholders and creditors (depositors) of a failed bank will eat the shortfall.

We have already seen this put into operation in other countries. Do you remember the panic in Cyprus that unfolded in March of 2013?[ii] Some of the major banks in Cyprus—which is an island in the Mediterranean that has served as a tax haven for world investors—had invested in Greek government debt. When that turned out to be a bad bet, international officials proposed a rescue plan that involved levying a fee on *all* savings accounts in Cyprus to cover the loss. Naturally, the regular people of Cyprus panicked when they caught wind of the plan, and wanted to withdraw their money from the banks. So the government *shut down* the banks, and imposed limits on ATM withdrawals. Some people couldn't access their money for more than a week. Ultimately there was immense public outrage and so the average person was spared, but large depositors had their accounts clipped, and they were given an IOU or in some cases shares of stock in a bank that was bankrupt. Imagine trying to make your payroll with *that*.

Now at this point, American readers are likely to ask, "But what about FDIC? Isn't my money in the bank backed up by a reserve fund?"

In principle, yes, but let's run the numbers. As of the second quarter in 2017, the FDIC had $88 billion in funds available to "make whole" the depositors with guaranteed accounts, in case their banks went under. That sounds like a lot of money, doesn't it? However, consider that there are some *$7.1 trillion* in total insured deposits that FDIC is "backing up" with that reserve. In other words, according to the latest numbers as of this writing, FDIC has a reserve fund that covers only a little more than *1 percent* of insured bank deposits.[iii] And, as we've stressed, in any future bank crisis, the plan is for *no additional taxpayer money* to be used to rescue failing depository institutions.

It's also worth pointing out a fact that many Americans don't realize. In the year following the financial crisis that struck in the fall of 2008, the FDIC's official fund balance stood at *negative* $8 billion by September 2009.[iv] Now to be clear, no American depositors lost money from failed banks in this episode, and at the time a panic didn't occur, because the FDIC could tap a credit line with the Treasury. Our point is that the government isn't magic. Just because it officially "guarantees" commercial bank deposits doesn't mean it will have the ability to do so, if and when the next major bank crisis hits. And now that Dodd-Frank is in force, as we explained earlier in this chapter, the U.S. government's official stance is that going forward, the Treasury will *not* kick in money to salvage failing banks.

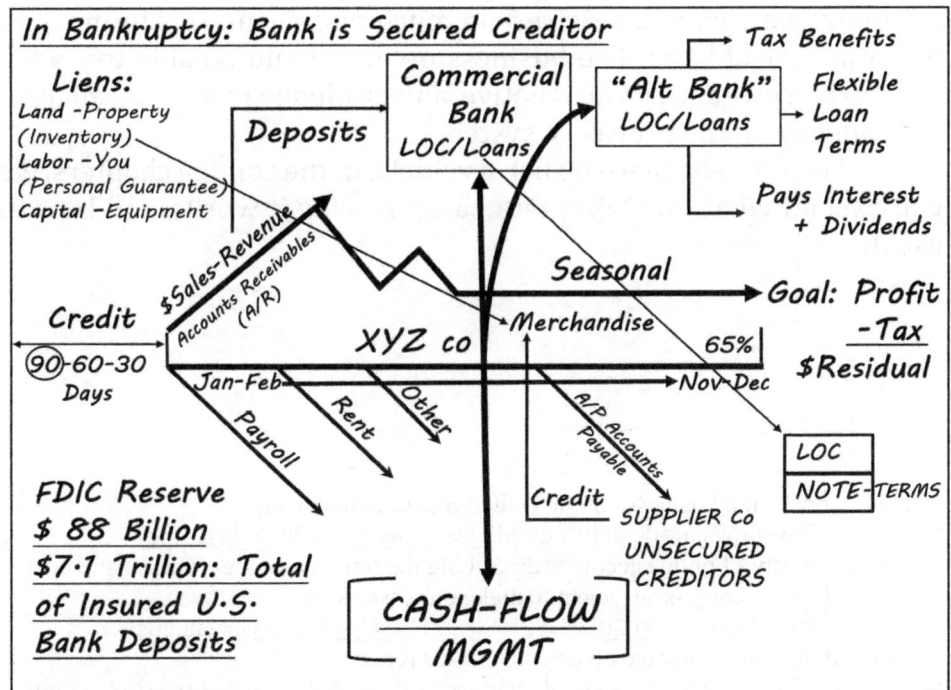

Conclusion

Now we've sketched out the financial problem facing the typical business owner. Because of his variable revenues and recurring expenses, he needs a source of funds to supplement his cashflow in tight months. Traditionally, commercial banks provided that feature through "convenient" lines of credit. But we saw the danger inherent in this approach, where a few bad months could spell the demise of a business.

We stress that most business owners don't realize the stranglehold that the commercial banks have on them...until it's too late. When times are good, the liens that come attached with the commercial bank Line of Credit aren't relevant. Yet if and when sales dry up, that's when the business owner realizes how much the deck is stacked against him.

If only there were an *alternate bank* that could provide cashflow management services, on much more generous terms than the commercial bank. The business owner would be able to sweep excess cash into such an alternative, and gradually wean himself from dependency on the prevalent system.

Fortunately, there *is* such a vehicle. In the coming chapters, we will explain what this "alternate bank" is, why it works, and how to use it.

---

[i] Statistics on "small business" in the United States available at:
https://www.sba.gov/sites/default/files/advocacy/SB-FAQ-2016_WEB.pdf.
[ii] There are plenty of online accounts describing the timeline of the Cyprus bank crisis, but the Wikipedia entry is sufficient to make our case. See:
https://en.wikipedia.org/wiki/2012%E2%80%9313_Cypriot_financial_crisis.
[iii] FDIC information available on page 23 of this report:
https://www.fdic.gov/bank/analytical/quarterly/2017-vol11-3/fdic-v11n3-2q2017.pdf.
[iv] See the FDIC press release of November 24, 2009, available at:
https://www.fdic.gov/news/news/press/2009/pr09212.html.

Chapter 2

The "Perfect Investment"

In the last chapter, we explained the precarious situation facing the business owner. We concluded that if only there were an "alternate bank" where he could direct any excess cash, that this would allow him to gradually begin weaning himself off of his reliance on commercial banks and their lines of credit.

As you know, the entire *purpose* of this book is to make "the case for IBC." Now fair warning: What we are going to say in the coming chapters runs against the conventional wisdom as espoused by the financial gurus on TV and the radio. To be sure, when the time comes we will address these common objections and concerns. Yet in our experience, it helps to do some additional preparation work on the front end. Before we dive into the details of IBC and how it operates, we are going to take the time for one more "warm up" exercise in this second chapter.

Specifically, we are going to ask you, the reader, to participate in a fun thought experiment. Don't worry right now about whether our discussion sounds realistic. Hypothetically speaking, what are the characteristics you'd want in an "ideal investment"? We know that in the real world every possible investment has one or more drawbacks, but if you could invent a type of asset from scratch that had *no* drawbacks, what would it look like?

In actual conversations with business owners, one of us (Carlos Lara) walks through this exercise, letting them volunteer the answers. They want to know where and how he invests his own money, so he turns their question around into a self-discovery exercise. Since this is a written book, obviously we will have to speak on behalf of you the reader, but you will see that our answers are quite straightforward.

Attributes of the "Perfect Investment"

If you were designing the perfect investment, what would it look like?

High Rate of Return The first thing most people say is that they want the market value of their investment to increase significantly over time.

Consistent Rate of Return When pressed, most people will further explain that not only is it desirable to have a high rate of return *on average*, but that if we're talking about the "perfect investment" we want that high rate of return to be *consistent*. In other words, if investment A and investment B both yielded (say) a 20% return per year over the course of ten years, people would prefer to hold the investment that was more predictable, year to year.

Conservative (Safe) This is a logical extension of the desire for consistency. People want an investment that only goes *up*: Once it reaches a particular market value, it can't go down from there.

Liquid It's one thing to know that your investment is "worth" a certain amount of money, but it's another to be able to *convert it into dollars* should the need arise. A liquid asset can be sold for its market value to raise cash very quickly.

Guaranteed Some assets come with actual guarantees put out by reputable and strong institutions, so naturally the "perfect investment" would too.

Tax Benefits (Tax Free) Ideally, our hypothetical investment would not significantly increase our tax liability. In a perfect world, we would enjoy all of its other benefits without suffering any tax consequences—the investment gains would be tax free.

No Market Volatility Now that we've hit the major items, people often circle back to the rate of return considerations. It's not just that they want this hypothetical investment to be dependable, but ideally it would not be tied to the performance of the stock market. This way, if and when the individual's *other* assets have a bad year, the "perfect investment" still has a predictable increase, which is all the more valuable in such a scenario.

Yields Income Besides Capital Gain The perfect investment would provide a cashflow over time, beyond its simple market appreciation in value.

Creditor Protected It's one thing to focus on the safety and guarantees propping up the market value of the asset we're studying, but to make it even *more* desirable the owner would enjoy creditor protection. In other words, if the owner of our hypothetical investment got into trouble elsewhere, and owed outsiders more than he could pay them, these creditors would *not* be able to seize his "perfect investment." (That's part of what makes it perfect.)

Inflation Protection This is similar to "no market volatility." Just as the investor wouldn't want this hypothetical asset to drop when the stock market crashes, on the other hand we want our perfect investment to increase in value to keep pace with price inflation.

Control This is related to "liquid." People are very familiar with investments that they have no control over; their money is being held by others and is effectively in prison, perhaps for decades. The ideal investment would not be locked up behind onerous penalties for "early withdrawal."

Transferable If desired, the owner should be able to easily transfer ownership of the perfect investment to someone else.

Easy to Manage There shouldn't be a big "learning curve" to figure out how to make decisions with the perfect investment. Not only does the owner want to be in control, but that control shouldn't come with headaches.

No Hidden Fees or Penalties Many people have been burned enough times by institutional money management firms that promote impressive rates of return in their brochures, without making it clear how much of those returns are absorbed by the management fees. The perfect investment would be very transparent so that the owner would never be surprised by money taken off the top.

Reputable At this stage in the conversation, many people begin squirming. "Carlos," they protest, "we want this thing to be *legal*, right?" So in addition to all of the attributes we've described so far, it would also be ideal if our investment were reputable.

Private The perfect investment, though reputable, would also be *private*. Your tax person wouldn't be getting 1099s every year, explaining the performance of your investment and otherwise telling people about your business.

We can wrap up our spit-balling session at this point. Perhaps you, the reader, can think of some more attributes of the hypothetical "perfect investment," but surely we've done a fair job summarizing the most obvious features.

Surprise!

At this point in his typical meeting, Carlos is ready to let the cat out of the bag: He informs the business owner (who had earlier asked Carlos where *he* puts *his* money) that this list of attributes that the business owner volunteered comes pretty close to describing a dividend-paying Whole Life insurance policy! Naturally, the person is often floored. "Why, I've always heard that this was the *worst* place to put your money!?"

Best of all, we haven't even shown you yet what you can do when you "become your own banker." We are simply talking about the standard attributes of a dividend-paying Whole Life policy.

In case you, the reader, are skeptical, it might help to use the above list of criteria in reference to *other* types of assets first. Once you see the pros and cons of the other places where the gurus have no problem, it may dawn on you that the conventional wisdom regarding Whole Life is uninformed.

The Pros and Cons of Various Asset Classes

To be sure, in this fallen world, *there is no such thing* as a truly "perfect investment." Instead, for various types of assets, we can simply identify which of the features (from our above list) that they do well on, and which of the features they fail to satisfy.

Let's start with an obvious type of investment: the stock market. The advantage of stocks is that they enjoy a relatively high rate of return *on average, over long periods of time*. They are also very liquid; you can call your broker and turn your stock holdings into "cash in the bank" by the end of the day. Furthermore, if you own stocks that pay dividends, then you can also enjoy a flow of income beyond the appreciation in market value. On the negative side, though, stocks are very volatile—they can crash 22 percent in a *single day*, as Americans witnessed during "Black Monday" in October 1987. Furthermore, if you want to enjoy tax benefits, then you will have to run your stock holdings through a tax-qualified plan such as a 401(k), 403(b), IRA, etc., where there are strict limits on when you can access your money (if you want to avoid penalties).

Another popular investment are bonds. They share many of the features of stocks, except that bonds tend to be safer. (This makes sense, because a corporation must first use its revenue to pay bondholders, before distributing any residual to the stockholders.) However, offsetting this advantage of safety is that bonds tend not to appreciate in value as rapidly as equities (another name for stocks). Also, because they are "fixed income"—meaning that the bond promises a flow of dollars—bonds are poor assets during periods of unexpected and rapid price inflation. In contrast, stocks are claims on ownership of the corporation itself, so that if (say) all prices in the economy are rising rapidly, then your stocks should rise on that account too.

What about <u>real estate</u>? Owning rental properties (either commercial or residential) can be very attractive, because property values tend to rise and so long as you can find tenants, you earn a consistent flow of rental income. However, even though people *used* to think that "houses always go up," that is obviously not true during major crises such as the Great Depression, the real estate crash in the 1980s, and of course the bursting of the housing bubble in the mid-2000s. Another downside of real estate is its lack of liquidity. Even in a normal, rising market, it might take a month or more (depending on the time of year, city, and neighborhood involved) to turn your "property that's worth $350,000" into an actual $350,000 in your checking account, not to mention the commission earned by the realtor. If you have an emergency come up and need access to your wealth, having it locked up in the form of real estate will be a disadvantage.

What about the precious metals, <u>gold and silver</u>? (These would often be classified under the heading "commodities" in a typical discussion about asset classes.) Historically gold and silver were the two examples of "commodity money" that the market voluntarily chose, as Lara and Murphy explained in their previous book, *How Privatized Banking* **Really** *Works*. As such, to this day investors flock to gold and silver as a "safe haven" during crises. In our age of government-issued "fiat money," the chief virtue of gold and silver is service as an "inflation hedge," meaning that these assets not only keep pace with a depreciating dollar (or euro, yen, etc.), but actually *more than* compensate when paper currencies fall rapidly. Moreover, for people who value privacy, control, and ease, it doesn't get much better than having a bag of gold coins in your house safe. However, there are downsides with the precious metals, considered as an asset class. Their market value can be quite volatile: After performing very well in the late 1970s, gold crashed in the early

1980s. Furthermore, the precious metals don't generate a flow of income; you would have to sell off portions of your holdings, if you used gold as a way to save for your children's college or to take vacations later in life. There is also the problem of liquidity, where the individual investor has to pay fees buying and selling.

Just to round out our discussion, what about keeping your wealth in the form of "cash," whether in the slang sense of money market mutual funds (MMMFs) or literally as deposits in checking or savings accounts with commercial banks? The supreme advantage of "cash" is liquidity—indeed we have been rating other asset types above, by how fast you can turn their market value *into* cash in your bank account. Another obvious advantage of "cash" as an asset is its (relative) safety and guarantees; you don't expect the market value of your property to go *down* (as measured in dollars) in your money market fund or your checking account. Of course, nothing in this world is truly guaranteed; the Reserve Primary Fund "broke the buck" in the fall 2008 crisis, thousands of commercial banks failed during the Great Depression, and even now FDIC doesn't provide an adequate safety net if things really turn south (as we explained in the last chapter). But even granting the liquidity and relative safety of "cash" as an asset class, the obvious drawback is that it earns a piddling rate of return. This is why most investors only have a small portion of their overall portfolio in the form of "cash," except in times of extreme uncertainty.

Whole Life Insurance as the "Captain Kirk" of Assets

We just walked through the major types of investments that the gurus will recommend when it comes to "retirement planning." Compared to our list of attributes for the "perfect investment," we saw that in the real world, any particular investment has strengths and weaknesses. Different investors will care more about some of our attributes than others, and therefore they would prefer to have a larger fraction of their total wealth held in the form of certain assets versus others. There's no necessarily right or wrong answer that an outsider could dictate: A middle-aged lawyer who is very worried about the dollar crashing might have large holdings of gold coins and foreign real estate, while a retired construction worker might have all of his wealth in the form of a paid-off house and annuities.

In this context, we circle back to our earlier claim—which may have seemed quite bold at the time: Our list of attributes of the hypothetical "perfect investment" comes very close to describing a dividend-paying—sometimes called a "participating"—Whole Life insurance policy, preferably issued by a mutual company. (A mutual company is owned by the policyholders, whereas a stock life insurance company is owned by third-party investors.)

For some readers, it might help if we use an analogy and describe Whole Life as the "Captain Kirk" of assets. What we mean by this is that Whole Life does very well on just about all of the criteria we listed above, and even where it's weak, it's not all *that* weak. Our reference here is the classic TV show *Star Trek*, where the Captain was the most well-rounded and consequently the one who would be the best to deal with a generic crisis. Sure, the Vulcan Mr. Spock was smarter and stronger, Dr. McCoy was better at healing an injury, and Scotty knew more about engineering. But in general, Kirk was pretty good at everything and had no serious deficiencies, which is why *he* was the Captain.

In the coming chapters, we will explain in detail exactly how *and why* a properly-designed Whole Life policy can fulfill so many of our desired objectives that we listed earlier in this chapter. But for now, let us state for the record that it is safe, private, liquid, guaranteed, reputable, creditor-protected in certain states, easy to manage and transfer to others, provides a flow of dividends, is shielded from exposure to the stock market, enjoys many tax benefits, gives control to the individual, and carries no hidden fees. Indeed its "score" on these attributes rivals just about any of the other types of popular assets we discussed earlier.

On the downside, the major strike here is that the "cash value" of a Whole Life insurance policy has a lower internal rate of return than assets such as stocks and real estate. However, even here, the performance isn't *that* bad. Especially when you take into account the fact that a (properly structured) Whole Life policy's internal growth can be effectively tax free, the return is modest but respectable. And remember: Once your Whole Life policy reaches a certain market value, it *can't go down*. It can only go up. Also, keep in mind that we are talking about *life insurance*. If you pay one month's premium and then die, your beneficiary gets the full death benefit. The "rate of return on your investment" in such a scenario is enormous.

Another weak point for Whole Life is that it is dollar-denominated, meaning that in a high price inflation environment, it will not perform as well as other assets such as gold. However, even here, Whole Life is not *that* bad. For one thing, your *premium payments* are denominated in dollars also, so that your contributions into the policy are also weakening. To repeat, we are talking about life insurance, *not* bonds (even though the life insurance company invests primarily in bonds). In addition, over time the life insurance company rolls over its bond portfolio, so that the higher interest rates (which would go hand in hand with higher price inflation) would eventually allow for the payment of greater dividends to the life insurance policyholders.

In sum, a dividend-paying Whole Life insurance policy, preferably issued by a mutual company, is a very robust financial asset. In reference to our list of the attributes of a "perfect investment," a Whole Life policy does very well on just about all of the criteria, while falling short on only two—and even there, it's not as bad on these two criteria as standard bonds or "cash." Yet nobody says, "Only a fool would put his wealth in cash."

In the coming chapters we will explain much more fully how Whole Life policies work, and why they are able to perform as we've described above. The purpose of our discussion in this chapter was simply to place the coming material in the proper context, and to defuse the knee-jerk reaction that we often encounter when trying to explain IBC to newcomers. As this chapter has hopefully convinced you, there's nothing "crazy" about incorporating a Whole Life policy into one's mix of assets, even *before* we start talking about IBC!

IBC Is a Process, Not a Product or Investment

To conclude this chapter, we should emphasize that IBC is a process, not a product. We used the phrase "perfect investment" for rhetorical effect, but to be clear, Nelson Nash is *not* advising people, "I think you should invest less in real estate / stocks / gold, and more in Whole Life." Rather, IBC is a process of "becoming your own banker," and a dividend-paying Whole Life policy is the best vehicle for implementing it.

It is necessary to defuse the knee-jerk reaction many people have to Whole Life, since (after all) it *is* the platform for implementing IBC. Remember last chapter, when we demonstrated the business owner's need for an "alternate bank"? Well, this is it: A properly structured, dividend-paying Whole Life policy is what we will use (in the coming chapters) to solve the business owner's economic problem.

As we've seen in this chapter, even a standard Whole Life policy on its own terms is a robust asset; it's no wonder it used to be a crucial component of many households' savings. Yet Nelson Nash discovered that this conservative, workhorse asset could be used in a powerful way to achieve much more. Over the course of this book, we will explain his discovery and how you can use it in your business or household.

Chapter 3

Banking and Life Insurance:

Process versus Platform

In Chapter 1 we described the precarious condition of the average business owner, and demonstrated the need for an "alternate bank" to reduce the reliance on lines of credit advanced by commercial banks. In Chapter 2 we listed attributes of a hypothetical "perfect investment," and then revealed—perhaps to your surprise!—that we had come close to describing a dividend-paying Whole Life insurance policy. In the *next* chapter, we are going to explain how you can "become your own banker," in the way that Nelson Nash explained in his classic book. But right now, in *this* chapter, we will provide the transition. In order for you to appreciate Nash's new approach to banking that we'll lay out in Chapter 4, you first need to understand the basic mechanics of a Whole Life insurance contract.

Fundamentally, Nelson Nash teaches people to take control of the banking function in their households and businesses. After all, the Infinite Banking Concept (IBC) has "banking" right in the title. However, the best way to *implement* IBC is to use one or more specially designed Whole Life policies. Banking is the *process*, while life insurance is the *platform*.

We don't need to get too deep into the weeds, but in this chapter we will give you the information you need to make sense of Nash's revolutionary concept.

Life Insurance: Term vs. Permanent

Everybody is familiar with term life insurance, because it operates much like other types of insurance (car, fire, homeowners, etc.). For example, if you take out a 10-year term life insurance policy with a $200,000 death benefit, the insurance company will quote you a "level" premium meaning how much you have to pay every month during the entire ten years. So long as you keep paying that fixed dollar amount each month, then your term policy remains "in force," and if the insured person happens to die, then the insurance company sends a $200,000 check to the beneficiaries named in the policy. On the other hand, if the ten years comes and goes and the insured party is still *alive*, then the contract ends. At that point, you can try to take out *another* life insurance policy on the same person (who could be yourself), but now the person is ten years older and so the premium for a subsequent term policy will be higher than it was for the original one. Furthermore, if the insured party has developed a medical condition (such as heart trouble, cancer, etc.) during the original term, then once that first policy expires, he or she may be deemed uninsurable.

In contrast, a *permanent* life insurance policy doesn't have a built-in expiration date. As its title suggests, a permanent policy stays "in force" permanently, so long as the policyholder continues to make the contractually required premium payments. Even if the insured party develops a serious medical condition down the road, the policy cannot be dropped and it never expires. So long as the premiums keep coming in, the life insurance company will definitely have to pay out the death benefit claim at some point, because eventually the insured party is going to die. (There is a subtlety here, in that policies can also "mature" or "endow" when the insured person becomes quite old, for example 121 years. In this case, the insurance company sends the check even though no death has occurred. But either way, the insurance company will eventually pay out on a permanent life insurance policy that is kept in force.)

Another common label for permanent life insurance policies is "cash-value life insurance." Unlike a typical term policy, where the customer is buying "pure" death benefit coverage for a unit of time, with a permanent policy there is an added element of a growing financial asset. Over time, a permanent life insurance policy has a growing "cash value" that the policyholder can access in various ways. (We will explain this more, later in the chapter.) A common analogy to explain the distinction is to say that term life insurance is like renting an apartment: you pay your monthly rent to the landlord, in exchange for one month's worth of "shelter services." But you don't build up ownership in the apartment. In contrast, if you take out a mortgage to buy an apartment unit, then with each monthly payment you are gaining equity in the property. Your monthly payment is not merely gaining you a month's worth of shelter, but it is also building up a valuable financial asset that you own.

Now that we've explained the basic difference between a term and permanent life insurance policy, in the next section we explain that there are different *types* of permanent life insurance products.

"Whole Life" versus Other Permanent Products

The plain vanilla, "old school" example of permanent (or cash-value) life insurance is the **Whole Life policy**. It has been around for more than a century, and was the standard vehicle by which Americans saved using life insurance. (We give more of the history of life insurance in Chapter 6.) *This* is the vehicle that Nelson Nash recommends as ideal for practicing IBC.

When you take out a Whole Life insurance policy, there is an initial death benefit and a level premium, which must be paid for a specified period. One approach is to configure the policy so that you must make premium payments until you die. Or, you might have it designed so that after you reach age 100—if you're still alive—then you no longer have to make premium payments; it is "paid up at 100" and the policy remains in force, even though you are no longer contributing money into the policy. Naturally, the *size* of the required premium (for a given death benefit) will vary, depending on your choice of the premium schedule. If you elect for a "paid up at 65" policy with $500,000 in death benefit coverage, then the premium you have to pay through your 65th birthday will be higher, than if you opt for a "paid up at 100" policy with a $500,000 death benefit, and you could make the premium lower still if you have a policy that is *never* paid up (i.e. it requires premium payments so long as you are alive[i]). The appropriate premium schedule isn't based on gaming the system, but instead involves your expected financial position over the course of your life, and whether you want to "pre-pay" certain expenses.[ii]

In addition to having a fixed premium payment that will guarantee a specified death benefit for the rest of your life, the standard Whole Life policy also includes guaranteed "cash surrender value" minimums, over the life of the policy. In other words, when you sign the contract for a Whole Life policy, you can see a schedule (for each year in the future) of the minimum lump-sum cash payment that you will be paid, if you should decide to cancel the policy down the road. We will explain this feature in more depth later in this chapter, and then even more so in Chapter 5, but for right now, you should realize that the cash surrender feature makes perfect sense: Because the premium on a Whole Life policy is much higher than for a *term* policy with the same death benefit, with no cash surrender feature there would be a risk in taking out a Whole Life policy, paying its higher premiums for (say) 20 years, and then having financial trouble and dropping the policy. This risk is mitigated by the ability of a person to receive a cash payment upon surrender of the Whole Life policy, which at least partially compensates for the "overpayment" on premiums (relative to a term policy) up to that point. After all, the life insurance company has been taking those relatively high premium payments and "putting them to work" by buying financial assets, and so the company is able to give you a lump-sum payment (which grows over time) should you decide to surrender the policy after you are years into it.

Another important feature of a Whole Life policy is the *dividend payments*. When setting the (fixed) premium for a Whole Life policy, the insurance company is very conservative. That is, they collect premiums that are actually higher than what the actuaries and other experts project will probably be necessary, in order to hit the guaranteed minimum cash surrender targets, and to pay out the death benefit when the insured person dies. Over time, therefore, the life insurance company will probably have excess assets on its books, earmarked to "back up" a particular block of Whole Life policies that it issued in the past. In a typical year, the insurance company will return some of the past premiums that, in retrospect, it didn't need to collect from the policyholders. These payments are called *dividends* for obvious reasons, though, strictly speaking, for tax and accounting purposes they are not the same thing as dividends paid on shares of stock.

When receiving dividends on a Whole Life policy, the policyholder has several options. First, he can get a check and effectively take the money out of the hands of the insurance company. Second, he can tell the insurance company to hang on to the money, by rolling the dividends into a "side fund" of conservative bonds. Third, he can instruct the insurance company to use the dividends in order to buy fully paid up, additional life insurance. (This is the standard move that you would use when practicing IBC.) This choice will recycle your dividends back into the policy, causing a jump in the cash value and death benefit.

There are many additional features and possibilities with a Whole Life policy; we will explore some of them in the coming chapters, to see how it can be optimized for IBC. But at this point, we've explained enough about a Whole Life policy so that we can contrast it with the newer product types. Unlike the classic Whole Life policy—which has been around longer than the automobile—these newer products came into vogue in the late 1970s and 1980s, in an era of high price inflation and interest rates. (We give more of the history in Chapter 6.) Let us stress that **Nelson Nash developed IBC for use with a Whole Life policy**, *and he strongly discourages anyone from attempting to "bank" with other products.* Indeed, we feel so strongly about this that our Authorized IBC Practitioners are strictly forbidden from setting up an IBC policy using anything other than a Whole Life policy. Nevertheless, in the interest of educating you the reader and providing context, we will briefly describe other types of life insurance products that can also be classified as "permanent" or "cash-value."

A Universal Life (UL) policy, at least in its plain vanilla form, is very similar conceptually to a Whole Life policy. The idea was to unpack the different components of a Whole Life policy, and then give the policyholder the ability to "change the dials" as it were. For example, with a UL policy, the policyholder can reduce the death benefit. (This might make sense for a couple with a mortgage. Each year, the remaining principal is lower, and so the couple might reduce the death benefit coverage on the life insurance policy, since its major function is to knock out the mortgage in case the breadwinner dies.) A UL policy also allows the user to set the premium. As time passes, the UL policy is updated based on the performance of the insurance company's portfolio of assets, death benefit claims, etc. Unlike a Whole Life policy, where all of the different factors are handled "under the hood," with a UL policy the goal was transparency, so that the policyholder could see all of the moving parts that affected how much cash was available at any given time. Since a Whole Life insurance policy functions as both "pure" death benefit coverage as well as a financial vehicle, the idea behind UL was to separate those functions and provide information on each component to the user.

Other permanent life insurance products are variants of the basic UL. For example, Variable Universal Life (VUL) has the flexibility of regular UL, but also allows the user to "invest" her side fund in various accounts, including ones that consist of stocks. Another product is Equity Indexed Universal Life (EIUL), which (as the name suggests) ties the growth of the cash value to a stock market index, but which can also offer downside protection in the event of a market crash.

We are not here to praise or disparage other types of life insurance products. But let us emphatically repeat: *It is a mistake to implement IBC with anything other than a dividend-paying Whole Life policy.* The whole *point* of IBC is to effectively secede from the volatile system centered on Wall Street and the commercial banking system.

A Whole Life policy is a conservative financial product with guarantees that protect the policyholder; the risk is borne by the insurance company. In order to gain "flexibility" and "participate in the gains" of the stock market, the other types of permanent life insurance expose the individual to more risk. Even with a standard UL policy (which is not tied to the stock market), if interest rates change, the policy might end up "eating itself away" while an inattentive owner doesn't realize it. In the real world, there have been

Banking and Life Insurance: Process vs. Platform

many horror stories of people leaving their UL policy in a drawer and then getting a letter from the insurance company warning that it was about to collapse.

To repeat, this type of surprise doesn't happen with a Whole Life policy, which is why Whole Life is the appropriate choice when picking a place to serve as your "alternate bank."

How to Read a Whole Life Policy Illustration

In the previous section, we outlined some of the basic features of a Whole Life policy. In this section, we will walk through a hypothetical illustration of such a policy, to drive home the concepts as well as to help you interpret actual illustrations in the real world.

The following table is closely based on an actual Whole Life insurance policy illustration circa 2013.

The policy depicted in the table is for a 35-year-old man. It is a "paid up at 90" Whole Life policy, meaning that the man owes the contractual premium—which is the same dollar figure throughout the entire period—through his 90th birthday, after which time he owes no additional money to keep the policy in force. (You can see in the second column of the table that the $10,000 premium drops to $0 when the man turns 91.)

Table 1. "Paid Up at 90" Whole Life Policy Illustration for 35-Year-Old (circa 2013)

Age	Annual Premium	Guaranteed Values Cash Surrender Value	NON-GUARANTEED PROJECTIONS			Death Benefit
			Annual Dividend	Net Premium Outlay	Cash Surrender Value	
36	$10,000	$0	$0	$10,000	$0	$776,000
37	$10,000	$3,100	$300	$9,700	$3,100	$776,000
38	$10,000	$12,500	$460	$9,540	$12,500	$776,000
39	$10,000	$22,000	$600	$9,400	$22,000	$776,000
40	$10,000	$32,000	$760	$9,240	$32,000	$776,000
41	$10,000	$41,000	$960	$9,040	$41,000	$776,000
42	$10,000	$50,000	$1,100	$8,900	$50,000	$776,000
43	$10,000	$59,000	$1,300	$8,700	$59,000	$776,000
44	$10,000	$69,000	$1,500	$8,500	$69,000	$776,000
45	$10,000	$79,000	$1,700	$8,300	$79,000	$776,000
...	...	...	...	...	...	...
72	$10,000	$427,000	$9,400	$600	$427,000	$776,000
73	$10,000	$442,000	$9,900	$100	$442,000	$776,000
74	$10,000	$457,000	$10,300	-($300)	$457,000	$776,000
75	$10,000	$471,000	$10,700	-($700)	$471,000	$776,000
...	...	...	...	...	...	...
89	$10,000	$659,000	$15,000	-($5,000)	$659,000	$776,000
90	$10,000	$673,000	$14,600	-($4,600)	$673,000	$776,000
91	$0	$679,000	$12,500	-($12,500)	$679,000	$776,000
92	$0	$684,000	$12,400	-($12,400)	$684,000	$776,000

Now to avoid confusion, let us stress that in this particular illustration, *the owner of the policy is NOT buying additional paid-up insurance through the use of dividends or by paying extra premiums.* When using a Whole Life policy to implement IBC, typically you *would* adopt these practices. But since we are right now just trying to teach you how to read a policy illustration, it's easiest if we first hold the

Banking and Life Insurance: Process vs. Platform

death benefit constant. To repeat: In our plain vanilla, basic illustration here, we are consciously *not* rolling the dividends back into the policy, even though you generally *would* want to keep your dividends in the policy for best results.

This illustration is showing you the standard "chassis" of a Whole Life policy, which has a constant death benefit that is supported by the level premium payment, where the guaranteed cash surrender value gradually rises until it equals the (constant) death benefit in the final year when the policy "endows" (completes). As it turns out, this specific policy matures at age 121—when the guaranteed cash value reaches $776,000—though our excerpt above doesn't go down that far into the future. In this example, we have the policyholder drawing out the dividends as they accrue, so that the basic death benefit remains in place.

A typical life insurance illustration will depict "Guaranteed" values on the left, and non-guaranteed values on the right, which are driven by assumptions concerning the performance of the life insurance company. As the term suggests, the cash surrender values on the left side are contractually *guaranteed*—no matter how the insurance company's portfolio performs, so long as this man keeps making his $10,000 annual premium payments, he is legally entitled to the growing cash values indicated in the third column.

In contrast, the values on the right-hand side of the table are *projections* based on reasonable assumptions. So if you had to pick which of the two sets of numbers would be closer to reality, you would go for the right-hand side, bearing in mind that those values aren't contractually guaranteed.

Specifically, the driving force behind the right-hand side numbers is the assumption that *dividends* will be paid on the policy. In other words, the left-hand side shows the bare-bones guaranteed performance, even if no dividend is ever issued. However, in practice the life insurance company will tend to have a nice margin available after each year (because of its conservatism), and so will distribute some of the surplus to the policyholders in the form of dividends.

To repeat, for this plain vanilla, introductory illustration, we have the owner of the policy drawing out the dividends as they are issued. That is why the "cash surrender value" is the same under both the guaranteed and non-guaranteed headings. However, if we had flipped the switch to make this hypothetical policyholder roll his dividends back into the policy—by buying additional paid-up insurance in small bursts—then with each such infusion, there would have been an immediate jump in both the cash value and the death benefit on the non-guaranteed side of the illustration.

It's important to clarify something about the dividends: Even though they aren't guaranteed, *once they are issued*, a dividend can't be rescinded, even if you "keep it in the policy." Specifically, once you use a dividend to buy additional paid-up insurance and make your cash value jump above the guaranteed level for a particular year, from that point forward your cash value will be *permanently* higher than the original guaranteed floors. The (gross) cash surrender value in your policy *cannot go down*, it can only go up.[iii] If the life insurer has a good year and issues a dividend, and you then use the dividend to buy more paid-up insurance, they can't take that away from you in the future, even if they have a bad year.

There is one final column for us to discuss: the Net Premium Outlay. This column accounts for the fact that the policyholder (per our assumption in this particular scenario) is drawing out the dividends from the policy whenever they are issued. Therefore, even though the policy owner contractually must pay $10,000 into the policy each year (up through age 90), the amount *out of pocket* continues to shrink as the policy matures. For example, at age 39, the dividend is $600. Since the policyholder pays in $10,000, but then takes out a dividend of $600, on *net* he's really only contributing $9,400 out of pocket into the policy that year. And this is what the Net Premium Outlay column indicates for that age.

By age 73, the annual dividend is projected to be $9,900, meaning that the policyholder only needs to contribute $100 net into the policy to keep it in force. And then at age 74—which we've shaded—the dividend has actually outrun the premium payment. That's why the Net Premium Outlay is a *negative* number. The policyholder takes more out of the policy than he puts in that year (and every year going forward). And yet, notice that the cash value continues to grow, year after year, even though the policyholder is drawing a growing dividend even taking into account the premium. And of course, this pattern is turbocharged at age 91, when the contractual premium has been satisfied and the policy is officially "paid up." At this point, the dividends are the owner's, free and clear. That is why the Net Premium Outlay jumps to (negative) $12,500 in that year. Note that *still*, even though the policy is fully paid up and we have told the company to keep paying all of the dividends directly to the policyholder, the cash surrender value continues to rise, year after year, even from age 91 onward.

Before leaving this section, we want to stress yet again: the point of the illustration in the table above *was only to teach you how to read a life insurance illustration*. In general, you would *not* want to use a Whole Life policy in the way depicted in the illustration. (Specifically, you would usually want to reinvest your dividends into buying more life insurance. Even if you wanted to begin consuming dividends in the later years, for tax reasons at some point you would probably want to switch to taking out policy loans rather than more dividends. Again, we are not providing specific advice; every situation is unique and you should consult with someone from our list of Authorized IBC Practitioners.)

Finally, regarding the above illustration, we should point out that our hypothetical man does *not* need to come up with even the Net Premium Outlay out of pocket every year. For example, at age 45, the man owes $8,300 net into the policy, to keep it in force. (That's the $10,000 contractual premium, less the expected $1,700 dividend that year.) But suppose something comes up, and the man doesn't *have* $8,300 that year to fund his Whole Life policy? In that case, never fear: As the table shows, the man has $79,000 of available cash. This means the man can simply take out a *policy loan* for $8,300 in order to pay his (net) premium due. We explain the basics of policy loans in the next section.

Policy Loans

Before you learn how to "become your own banker" in the next chapter, you need to understand one more concept: the policy loan. Remember earlier we explained that in a Whole Life policy, as you continued to make premium payments, the "cash surrender value" would grow. This was reassuring to the policyholder, because it showed what the "exit strategy" would be, in case he had to cancel the policy for some reason after pouring so much money into it. And from the life insurance company's perspective, it would be *able* to offer more and more generous cash payments, the longer it had been able to invest the incoming premium payments into a growing stockpile of financial assets.

But if you think about it, it would be a shame if someone had been pumping premiums into a Whole Life policy for, say, 40 years, and then had a cash crunch in a particular month and couldn't afford the premium. It would be especially ludicrous if the person then had to surrender the policy outright, receiving a large sum of money, which would have been more than enough to cover the premium payment. This is an outcome that neither the individual nor the insurance company wants.

Fortunately, there is another option. As part of the standard contract you sign, a Whole Life policyholder is entitled to take out *loans from the insurance company*, at a specified interest rate, with the cash surrender value serving as the collateral. So if a woman has a policy with (say) $50,000 in cash surrender value, and because of a cash crunch she can't come up with the $800 premium, she doesn't need to cancel the policy. Instead, the insurance company will give her a loan—for $2,000 let's say—at the interest rate specified in her contract (perhaps it's based on a market index and works out to 5%). With the $2,000 loan, she is able to pay the premium this month and next month (with some extra money left over for her other needs), until she gets out of her cash crunch. Her life insurance policy is still in force—after all, she made the premium payments each month—meaning that she still has the death benefit, and her (gross) cash

Banking and Life Insurance: Process vs. Platform 37

surrender value is still growing. She didn't "take money out" of her policy. Instead, her policy is still doing what it does, but now she just has a $2,000 loan on the side, rolling over at 5% interest.

It is important for you to understand that policy loans are money that the insurance company lends to you. To repeat, this money does not "come out of your policy," and by the same token, when you pay *back* the policy loan, that money goes to the insurance company, not "into your policy."[iv] Your policy is *involved* in the whole operation, to be sure, but that's because your policy's cash surrender value is serving as the collateral on the loan.[v] We stress these points because some of the literature in this genre tells people they are "borrowing from yourself" or "paying yourself back," and while we understand what these authors mean by such terminology, without the appropriate context some members of the public might be confused.

Now if you are taking out a loan from the life insurance company, when do you have to pay it back? The answer is: whenever you want. Specifically, a policy loan begins growing at the contractually guaranteed interest rate the moment you receive it. If you decide to send a payment on the loan to the insurance company, they will reduce the outstanding balance accordingly.

However, you also have the freedom to *never* service your policy loan. It continues to grow, alongside your policy, serving as a lien against its cash surrender value. If you ever decide to surrender the policy, at that point the life insurance company first pays off the loan balance, and then gives you only the net remainder. Or, if the insured party dies, then out of the death benefit the insurance company first pays off the loan balance, and only sends the net remainder to the beneficiaries.

It may help you to understand how this all works if you consider that the life insurance company has to do *something* with the incoming premium payments from its policyholders. For example, the insurance company might use the revenues to buy Treasury or corporate bonds, or to invest in a local shopping center. An additional investment opportunity (from the company's perspective) is to lend money to policyholders at a specified interest rate. These loans are the safest investment possible, from the insurance company's point of view, because the company itself guarantees the collateral. Thus, in our example above, the insurance company earned a *guaranteed* 5% on its $2,000 investment, which would roll over as long as the borrower hadn't fully knocked out the loan.

You've Got the Tools, Now Learn How to Use Them

In this chapter we laid out the basic features of a Whole Life policy. In case you are skeptical, don't worry: We explain *why* they work in Chapter 5. But at this point, you have the tools you need to understand how to become your own banker. This is our subject in the next chapter.

---

[i] Our remarks about Whole Life always include the caveat that if you live to the maturity or endowment of the policy, then the policy completes even though you are still alive. So obviously, if you live to be 121, then you would collect the "death benefit" and would no longer owe premiums on the policy, even if it were designed to never be "paid up."

[ii] As we explain later in this chapter, even if you have a policy that contractually requires more premium payments, you don't *need* to pay those out-of-pocket, if the policy has a sufficient amount of internal cash value.

[iii] In the text we are referring to the *gross* cash surrender value that is the basic framework of your Whole Life policy. Now of course, if you borrow money from the insurance company with your cash surrender value serving as collateral, then the *net* cash surrender value available will be lower. But it's important to understand that you aren't "taking money out" of your Whole Life policy when you obtain a policy loan: the cash surrender value is still growing, while you may have a policy loan that is rolling over at interest too. We explain the mechanics of policy loans later on in the text.

[iv] To avoid confusion, sometimes in the IBC literature an author will advise an individual to "pay back" a greater amount on the policy loan, than the company actually requires. (Indeed, Nelson Nash himself gives this advice in *Becoming Your Own Banker*.) But strictly speaking, what happens there is that once the policy loan is paid back—to the company—then the additional "loan repayments" are actually handled as contributions for paid-up additional insurance. So *those* payments do indeed "go into your policy," but strictly speaking the life insurance company has already been paid back its policy loan.

[v] There are technical differences among different insurance carriers in the treatment of policy loans, especially as they may or may not affect dividend payments. An Authorized IBC Practitioner can provide more information, but this lies outside the scope of the present book.

Chapter 4

Becoming Your Own Banker

The original and still canonical case for IBC is in Nelson Nash's book, *Becoming Your Own Banker*. The present book is *not* intended as a substitute for his classic work. However, the current chapter will provide a succinct statement of some of the most important elements of Nash's message for the public.

Before diving in, a note about the specific numbers: We have retained the numerical examples in the form that Nelson Nash originally provided them, in his book and public lectures. Naturally, as of this writing interest rates are lower than when Nash developed his material. Yet nothing about the principles involved depends on the *level* of interest rates. Rather than constantly tinkering with the numbers—which will always be "out of date" within a short while after another update—we have opted to leave the numbers in this chapter in their historical form. However, the illustrations that we offer elsewhere in this book reflect more recent conditions in the economy and life insurance sector.

Thinking Properly About "Money" and "Banking"

Before we even begin the message of this chapter it is vital that you understand—and agree—that *money is not synonymous with wealth*. Wealth includes all of the material means by which we enjoy goods and services. Money is the medium of exchange *whereby we acquire all kinds of wealth*. Money is a commodity.

It is also vital that you understand—and agree—that when we discuss "banking" we are *not* talking about a commercial bank like the ones you see on the streets of any city. We're talking about a *concept—an idea conceived in the mind* using dividend-paying Whole Life insurance (preferably with a Mutual Life Insurance company) as the primary reservoir of your medium of exchange during your entire lifetime. Inter-generational planning and implementation of this concept can produce spectacular results.

But, the greatest attribute of this concept is that it is placing the banking function in life down at the you-and-me level where it really belongs. This is in contrast to the concept of central banking—the one that has caused so much conflict and misery in the world.

Money Flows Into and Out of Pools

Someone once made the comment that "If some authoritative power distributed all the money in the world equally among all the people in the world, within ten years' time 97% of all the money would be under the control of 3% of the people." We suppose that there is no way ever to measure the validity of such a statement, but most people would agree that it is probably close to the truth. Even if the proportions were somewhat moderated—say 75% of the money would be under the control of 25% of the people—why do you think that this phenomenon happens?

Perhaps some of the answer lies in the fact that most folks know next to nothing about the process of banking and its importance to their lives and their well-being. Banking is *the* most important business in the world! Without it, all business comes to a screeching halt. Whenever a business transaction takes place, money must flow from one party to another in a relatively short time or, otherwise, nothing takes place. That *flow of money must come from a supply source, a reservoir.* That is the essence of what the banking business is all about; someo*ne* or *some organization* has control of a pool of money that can (and must) flow, at a cost, to meet some need.

Money must *flow!* Otherwise it is worthless.

There is only *one pool* of money in the world. The fact that this pool is managed by any number of institutions (banks, insurance companies, and corporations) and *individuals* in various countries with various currency denominations is incidental. To argue otherwise would be the equivalent of someone looking at the globe and observing that the Amazon River in South America flows into the

Atlantic Ocean and commenting that "this has nothing to do with the Indian Ocean on the other side of the globe."

Nonsense! It is all part of a system. Observe that about 75% of the earth's surface is covered by water. The sun heats it up and some of it evaporates into the atmosphere causing wind currents. The currents take the water vapor around the earth and it precipitates out in the form of rain, sleet, snow, and hail—and somewhere along the way some of it *flows through all of us.* Without it we die! That makes it of vital importance. Pray tell, where does it ultimately end up? Right! Back in the oceans!

The banking business is somewhat like that. Money flows from the pool through our hands to meet our needs—but somewhere in the process it all ends up back into the banking system. It is all a matter of *"how much of the banking function do you own—and control—as it relates to your needs."* This book is all about how to create your own banking *system* so that *you can control 100% of your needs. Becoming your own banker*! Give it your close attention and it can make a radical improvement in your financial future.

Nelson Nash's Background

To understand the origin of this concept requires some explanation of what led one of us (i.e. Nelson Nash) to it. First of all, Nash is a Christian. He made that commitment when he was nine years old. Everything that he has said and written about IBC has *gone through that filter first.*

Next, Nash was educated as a forester, having graduated from the University of Georgia in 1952. A large portion of the root thought of this concept is coming from his study of forest finance—the fact that you are dealing with compound interest over a long period of time with no taxation on the build-up. The reverse fact is that you must make an investment and *you won't see any result* for a long time! In the forestry world you must think many years into the future. Nash worked as a forestry consultant for about 10 years.

It was in this arena that he became vividly aware that there was something fundamentally wrong going on in our country—it was the prevalence of socialism. At first, Nash knew very little about the subject, but soon he came face-to-face with the mental paralysis that accompanies this evil monster.

A series of events led Nash to discover the Austrian School of economic thought through the Foundation for Economic Education (FEE). This provided a perfect explanation to counter the other schools of economic thought that dominated the world.

And so, Nash's 60+ year study of Austrian Economics became a passion in early 1957. The founder of FEE was Leonard E. Read. He became Nash's personal friend and mentor. In fact, Nash was a Charter Member of The Leonard E. Read Society. (There are only 100 members.)

Without this Austrian Economics experience the Infinite Banking Concept would probably never have been born.

Some of the concept is coming from the life insurance business. Nash made a good living in life insurance sales for over 35 years. Knowing how dividend-paying life insurance works is an essential ingredient to it all. Most people have a minimal understanding of the subject, *including* people who make a living in life insurance.

Another element of Nash's background is that he has been an aviator for over 70 years as of this writing. He spent 28 of those years with Army National Guard fixed-wing (low & slow types). The balance of flying hours was in the civilian world. Nash has equal flying time in both categories for a total of 8,000+ hours. Believe it or not, this experience does bring a different perspective to what goes on in the world.

Finally, this concept of IBC was strongly influenced by Nash's experience in the real estate business. Timber is a form of real estate as well as the land on which it grows, so Nash has been around real estate for all his working life and developed a strong interest in the subject, studying many books on it. If you read these books, the central message is not about real estate at all—it is about the magic of *leverage!* Essentially, they all say, "Buy some real estate, borrow the money to pay for it (because you are *always* dealing with borrowed money—you either borrow money and pay interest, or you use your own money and give up interest that you could have earned), pay interest for a while, then sell the property. All you have given up is the interest you have paid out. That leverage is *wonderful!*"

That is all true—as long as things are going the way the "financial geniuses" describe it. But they *never* tell you what happens when the *lever goes the other way!* For a while, Nash made some money in the late '70s doing it the way the "geniuses" explained it. (Someone remarked that "financial genius is a *rising market.*") There were several successful ventures in a row and it looked like there was no end to this bonanza. Nash felt he could do no wrong! The ventures got bigger and bigger and he got more and more involved, buying a large number of acres of rural property.

And then Nash got into real estate development. With the profits from one small parcel, he and his wife went to Europe in 1977 and spent a month! Would you believe it—he still hasn't seen that property yet. And he did it all according to "the book by the financial geniuses"—leverage—other people's money! Just have your realtor find such a deal and attend to all the particulars for you —and then sell it for you! Marvelous!

There was no logical reason not to *expand.* And so Nash did. The interest rate (prime) at that time was 8%, but you must pay 1.5% over "prime" (now referred to as *base rate*), because the bankers are *not* lending you money because you have real estate—they are doing it because *they think you can make payments*! Why else would they require personal endorsement on the loan? And you must renew the notes every 90 days—at the current interest rate. Nash got accustomed to paying 9.5% and that was just normal. And then, along came 1981 and 1982. The prime rate rose and "peaked" at 21.5%! It stayed at that level for 18 months. Add 1.5% on top of that and you see his situation—23% interest on $500,000! That amounts to $67,500 of interest per year *that he had not been expecting to pay.*

Now when this type of calamity happens to you, what do you do? Go ask the "financial geniuses" who recommended that you do this, "What do I do, now?" *If you can find them*, they may mumble something about "selling the real estate." But, where do you find a *fool* that will buy it under those circumstances? Of course, everything will sell if you get the price low enough, but this might translate into enormous losses compared to your original investment.

It was this debacle that caused Nash to indulge in introspection. He asked himself, *"What led me into this intolerable situation?* How did I succumb to the siren song of financial nonsense? Ideas that did not meet the standards of my Christian upbringing?"

He realized he had been trapped by the early "success" we mentioned a few paragraphs above. And the teachings of MBA schools and the business magazines extolling the magic of leverage were also a contributing factor.

Couple this fact with the advent of those high interest rates in the early 1980s. Nash had known all about hyperinflation in Germany in the 1920s and the same sort of thing that happened in Argentina, just to name a few examples. But, this is America! This sort of stuff *can never* happen here! We have our Federal Reserve to protect us from such insanity!

How wrong Nash was! Just look at what has happened to our savings rate in our country since 1950:

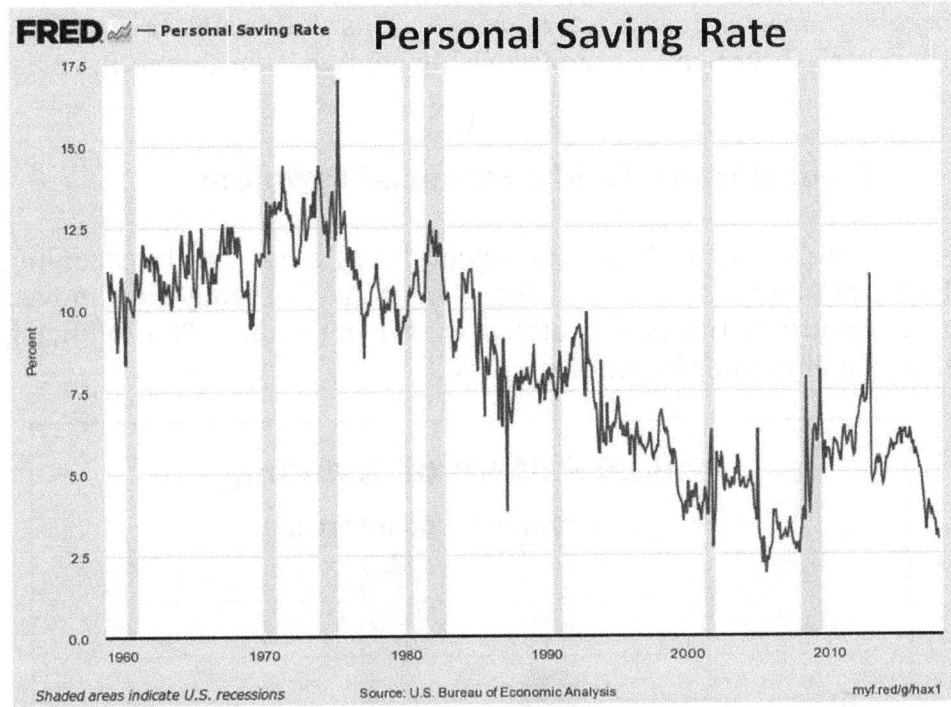

Sanity—and his study of Austrian Economics—led Nash to understand that *banks had created this problem*. People had come to think, "I don't need to save money; the banks are going to supply my need for the medium of exchange."

Nelson Nash's Fundamental Insight and Contribution

Based on Nash's background explained in the previous section, after his financial upheaval it dawned on him that people don't have to behave in the foolish way that he had. *They can secede from the way most of the world is behaving by understanding how dividend-paying Whole Life insurance works, and by realizing that this is the ideal place to warehouse your medium of exchange.*

When adopting this change in thinking—and utilizing this fantastic financial tool to solve the banking function—it is essential that you understand that *your need for finance during your lifetime is greater than your need for death benefit.* This simple statement is how Nelson Nash himself summarized his contribution to the financial world.

The Typical Household's Financial Problem

At one point, Nash did a good bit of study on the spending habits of American families. (The current numbers may have moved somewhat, but the basic pattern is still the same.) The following diagram illustrates his findings.

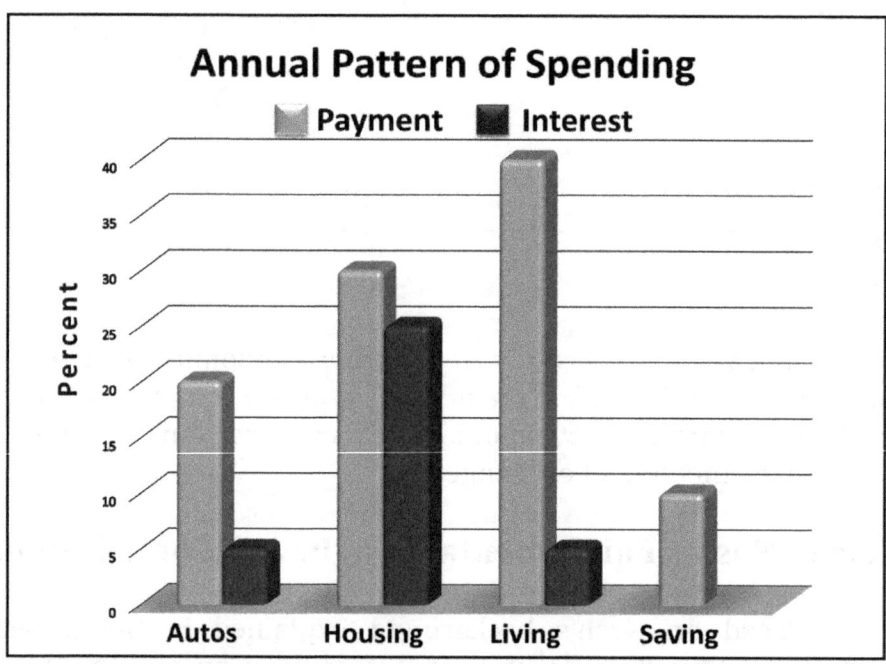

We often build scenarios around the "All-American family" because we don't want people to think you have to be rich to create a banking system that can handle all your needs for finance. This young man is 29 years old and is making $28,500 per year after taxes. What has the conventional banking system taught him to do? What does he do with the after-tax income?

Twenty percent is spent on transportation, thirty percent is spent on housing, and forty-five percent is spent on "living" (clothes, groceries, contributions to religious and charitable causes, boat payments, casualty insurance on cars, vacations, etc.). Many of these items are financed by charge cards or bank notes. The balance is *financed* by paying cash for them (and thus, giving up interest that could be earned, otherwise). He is saving less than five percent of disposable income. But, to be as generous as possible, let's assume that he is saving *ten percent* and spending only forty percent on living expenses. This is giving him every benefit of the doubt on the matter of savings. Just remember, the real situation is at least twice as bad as what will be depicted!

The problem is that all these items are *financed* by other banking organizations. An automobile financing package for this hypothetical person is $10,550 for 48 months with an interest rate of at least 8.5% with payments of $260.05 per month. But, if you will check with the sales manager of an automobile agency you will find that 95% of the cars that are traded in *are not paid for!* This means, at the end of 30 months, if the car is traded, 21% of every payment dollar is *interest*. Even if he goes the full four years, the portion of every payment made is still 20%! This means that the interest portion of every dollar spent is *perpetual*. It never seems to dawn that the *volume of interest* is the real issue, not the *annual percentage rate*. For a real thrill, go to see the sales manager of the high-priced cars and ask him what percentage of the cars that leave their car lot are *leased*. The answer will probably be 75%, or more! This is worse than financing a car purchase.

When you go to the Doctor's office to get a shot of some kind, the criterion is not the *rate* at which the medicine is injected into you—it is the *volume!* Too little, and it won't do any good—too much and it can kill you! The volume of interest is the problem, not the interest rate paid.

Now, let's move to the housing situation. This young man can qualify for a 30-year fixed-rate mortgage in the amount of about

$93,000 at a fixed interest rate of 7% APR with payments of $618.75 and closing costs of some $2,500. The problem is that within 5 years he will move to another city, move across town, or refinance the mortgage. Something happens to a mortgage within 5 years. Including the closing costs and interest paid out during these 60 months he had paid $39,625, but only $5,458 has gone to reduce the loan. This means that $34,167 has gone to interest and closing costs. Divide the amount paid out into the interest and closing costs and you find that *86% of every dollar paid out goes to the cost of financing!* If he sells the house in less than 5 years, it is worse. This proportion never gets any better because he takes on a new mortgage and starts all over again. He thinks that he is "buying" a house, but all he is really doing is making the wheels of the banking business and the real estate business turn.

In the next segment of his spending pattern—the living expenses—you will find that the interest on his boat payments, credit card interest, plus the cost of casualty insurance on the automobiles, etc. will rival in volume the interest he is paying on the purchase of the two automobiles.

Now, add up all the interest he is paying out and you find that 34.5 cents of every disposable dollar paid out is *interest*. For the average All-American male this proportion *never changes*. Let's assume that he is trying to save 10% of his disposable income, *which is twice the average savings rate in America*. That means that we have a 3.45 to 1 ratio of interest paid out as compared to savings. If you will get this young man together with his peers at a coffee break or some such gathering and have one of them suggest that they discuss financial matters, we can predict what they will talk about—getting a *high rate of return* on the portion they are saving! Meanwhile, every participant in the conversation is following the above financial strategy! What a tragedy! But that is how they have learned to conduct their financial affairs, courtesy of the banking community—and college finance courses.

This kind of thinking had its genesis many years ago but to see its movement over a long period requires that you read a lot of history on the subject. On our website, www.infinitebanking.org you will find a large History section that can get you started. For insight on this subject *in our modern times* you might recognize that it really began to blossom right after WWII and has gained momentum with time.

The Solution

So, how does one arrest—or better still, reverse—this trend? It's one thing to isolate the problem; what is the solution?

It is going to require introspection on your own part. Think things through! It will require you to *learn what nonsense looks like* and refrain from participating in it. No "knee-jerk" reactions to the advertising world.

You must learn that we deal with a medium of exchange called money to acquire goods and services from other people. You must learn to accumulate money in a location that has served mankind for longer than the USA has been a country. It is called dividend-paying Whole Life insurance, preferably with a mutual company—meaning one that is owned by the policy owners, as opposed to a "stock company" that has conventional shareholders. A Whole Life insurance policy is nothing more than a contract between like-minded people to solve a financial problem.

In summary, the accumulation of money (the act of banking) is a necessary function in our everyday lives. Without it there is no way that we can enjoy the standard of living that is ours. We would be living in caves! But, as we have cited above, the bankers have all but taken over the banking function in life and people have become "financial slaves."

The remedy for this deplorable situation *has to be done at the individual level.* It can't be done through "group thinking." So, *you* must learn how to *become your own banker.* It can be done in this hostile financial environment. You can live profitably while enjoying a peaceful, stress-free life style.

Understanding a Conventional Bank

Somehow or another, it never dawns on most financial gurus that you *can* control the financial environment in which you operate. Perhaps it is caused by lack of imagination, but whatever the cause, learning to control it is *the most profitable* thing that you can do over a lifetime.

If you are going to create a bank *like the ones you already know about*, there are a number of steps you must go through. You must first study the business so that you have a firm grip on what it is all about and feel that you can run such a business. Without this confidence you are fighting a lost cause. It's a jungle out there!

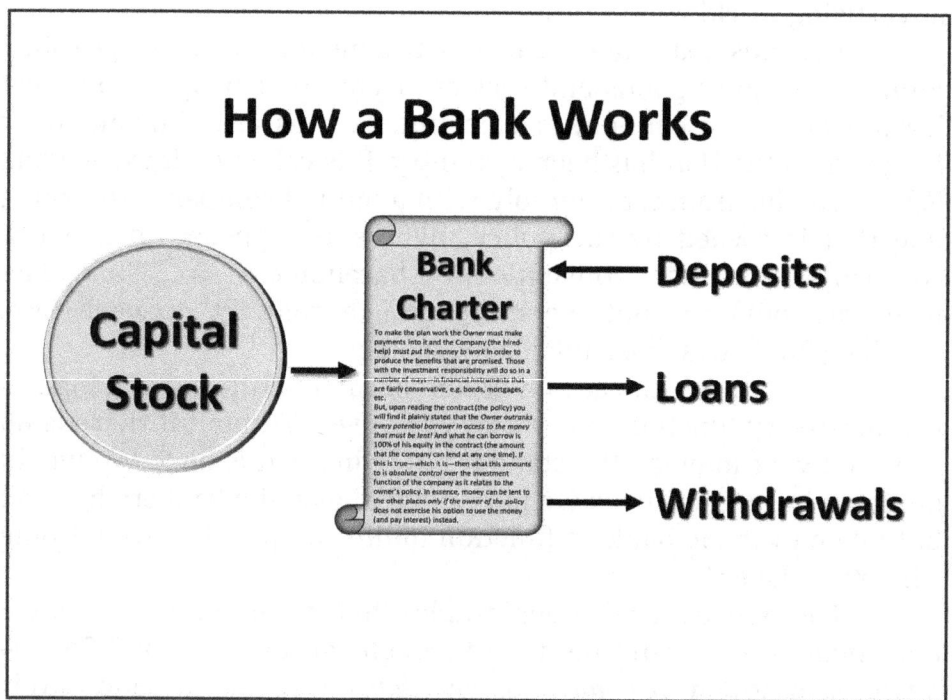

Next, you must get some capital—*money*—and it had better be in the order of $20 million or more. This money must sit in some other bank in a very liquid form, that is, it is earning a very low interest rate.

Then you go to the Banking Commissioner's office in your state and apply for a Bank Charter. Bear in mind that the Commissioner doesn't hand out charters indiscriminately. The chance of your getting one at this point is probably not very good. There are a lot of other folks that would like to be bankers. You must wait your turn. The bottom line is that you are going to spend a lot of time and money in this phase of creating your (conventional) bank. Years are likely to have passed before you finally win the coveted charter. In the meantime, you have probably gone through the part about a good location and suitable building, etc. This, too, is all at considerable expense.

Now you are finally in business as a bank. You must make your bank known by lots of advertising and inducing people to make deposits to your bank. Why do you think they would deposit their money with your bank when they could easily do business with established banks that have been there for years? Right! You are going to have to pay them something better than they are getting at their current banking connection. Do you notice, thus far, that you have been paying out money for years in getting this business established?

In his book, *Paper Money*, author Adam Smith (a modern author, not *the* Adam Smith) has this to say: *"A banker cannot make a loan unless he has a deposit. It seems a little silly to state that so baldly, but if three college-educated Americans in ten don't know that we have to import oil, I don't feel so bad about saying something bald. Banks do not lend their money. They lend the money somebody else has left there."* Later on in the book he goes on to explain: *"When you start up a bank, you have to put in some capital. Then you get some deposits, and then you lend the deposits. In a proper bank these three items bear a prudent relation to one another."*

Starting Your Own "Bank": A Better Way

You must admit that getting into the banking business in this conventional way is very costly and time consuming. It will be a long time before you show a profit—probably as much as ten years. But it must be extremely profitable over the long haul for people to go through the gory mess you have just read about.

There is a much easier way to accomplish the creation of your own banking system and the mechanism has been around for over 200 years. It is tried and true. It is called *participating (i.e. dividend-paying) Whole Life insurance.* But the problem is that very few people know how the business works, including the home-office folks in the life insurance companies!

To avoid confusion, let us stress: We are using the terms "bank" and "banking" in a broad sense, as opposed to a legal sense. For example, around Thanksgiving you might give canned goods to a *food bank.* During the winter, plows might create a *snow bank* on the roads. If you are a universal donor, you are encouraged to give to a *blood bank.* Closer to our usage, in a poker game the host might be "the bank" who holds the cash and hands out the chips. So when we talk about "setting up your own bank" or "becoming your own banker," we are speaking in this broad sense, rather than setting up an actual conventional bank as a legal entity. In terms of your actual financial "moves," you are simply starting a properly designed Whole Life policy and using its policy loan feature. But we are encouraging you to "think like a banker" when doing so.

Banking is all about accumulating money and making loans to people who will pay them back. You should be the ideal customer of your system. You should make loans to yourself—and pay them back. That way your accumulation of money is always growing in a continuous, unbroken pattern. It will always keep getting better. It cannot experience a reversal.

Remember this, because in the "banking system" we are going to tell you about, you can also destroy it by not obeying the basic rules of banking. *Loans have to be paid back or you can kill the best business in the world.* In other words, even though you have the *freedom* to take out a policy loan and never pay it back, you must realize that such a move comes with a cost. It's up to you, but don't try to blame others when your system doesn't live up to your expectations.

Co-Generation: Power and Banking

At this point, it will help if you understand what is meant by the word "co-generation." It is a term used in the production of electrical power. As most everyone knows electrical power is produced in plants primarily relying on fossil fuels, nuclear fuels, or water to turn turbines. But there is another source of electrical power that is significant—the wood-products plants—sawmills and paper mills. Trees are harvested for the wood they contain but the bark on the outside of the tree and the sawdust from sawing lumber has little economic value, but they make a very good fire! This source of heat can do the same thing that fossil fuels do to turn dynamos to produce electricity. Every sawmill of significant size and all paper mills have a "co-generation plant" to make their own electricity.

Imagine that you own a paper mill and that your co-generation plant can produce 500% of your mill's need for electrical power. What do you do with the surplus power? Yes, you can sell it. But, do you erect power distribution lines, get a sales force, etc. and ask potential customers if they would like to buy power from you instead of their customary power supplier? Heavens, no! You understand how the power distribution systems all work and simply tie into the established system and sell *them* the power. It is much more efficient than trying to do it any other way. Creating your own banking system through the use of dividend-paying Whole Life insurance is much like co-generation. All the ingredients are *already there in place*. All you have to do is understand what is going on in such insurance plans and tap into the system.

IBC: The Basics

To see the simplicity and effectiveness of the Infinite Banking Concept (IBC) there are some basic understandings that we must cover.

"Banking: The business of a bank, originally restricted to money changing, and now devoted to taking money on deposit subject to check or draft, loaning money and credit and any other associated form of general dealing in money or credit."
— Webster's Third New International Dictionary

The very first principle that must be understood is that you *finance* everything that you buy—you either pay interest to someone else, or you give up interest you could have earned otherwise. The alternate use of money must always be reckoned with. Some call this "opportunity cost." But, it is amazing how people give lip-service to this fact but do not put it into practice in their own financial dealings—the equivalent of thinking that the law of gravity applies to everyone else but them.

An excellent article appeared in the September 1993 issue of *Fortune* magazine, entitled, "The Real Key To Creating Wealth" by Shawn Tully, in which he describes the concept of Economic Value Added (EVA) developed by Stern Stewart & Co. of New York City. Tully says,

> Understanding that while EVA is easily today's leading idea in corporate finance and one of the most talked about in business, it is far from the newest. On the contrary: Earning more than the cost of capital is about the oldest idea in enterprise. But just as Greece's glories were forgotten in the Dark Ages, to be rediscovered in the Renaissance, so the idea behind EVA has often been lost in ever-darker muddles of accounting. Managers and investors who come upon it act as if they have seen a revelation.

In summary, before being introduced to EVA, corporations were borrowing capital from banks and paying interest—but they were treating their own capital (equity) *as if it had no cost!* When they were brought face-to-face with the error of their ways and conducted their business with this fact included in the equation, then the profitability increased dramatically. EVA's basic premise is this: If you know what's really happening, you'll know what to do. The same thing applies to *The Infinite Banking Concept.*

In creating any product, it all begins with engineering. The automobile you drive started out being "lines on a piece of paper." If the production workers don't do what the engineers designed, you won't have an automobile, but they did, and your car rolls off the assembly line. Suppose that someone gets the next one and it is "identical" to yours—same color, equipment, features, etc.—they are identical in every way. Can you safely predict that they will both *perform identically* during their lifetimes? Of course not! Because we all know someone who can get 200 to 300 thousand miles out of a car with no trouble. But, we also know some people who can't get 50 thousand miles out of their car before it is "worn out"! How you drive the car and care for it is far more important than anything else. Keep this thought in mind as we look further at the life insurance product.

The engineers in life insurance are known as "actuaries." They are dealing with a field of 10 million selected lives—persons who have been through a screening process. And they are working with a theoretical life span of 121 years. Then they turn their information over to "rate makers" who determine what the company is going to have to charge its clients in order to be able to pay the death claims and make the whole system work over a long period of time.

Then the whole matter is turned over to lawyers who make legal and binding contracts that are to be offered to potential buyers through a sales force. The glue that holds this all together is comprised of the administrative folks, executives and clerks, etc. The contract is unilateral—that is, the company promises to do certain things *if you meet the standards of acceptability and make premium payments.* **Read the contract and it will tell you very plainly that you are the owner of the contract**—not the company. **The Owner is the most important character in the scene.**

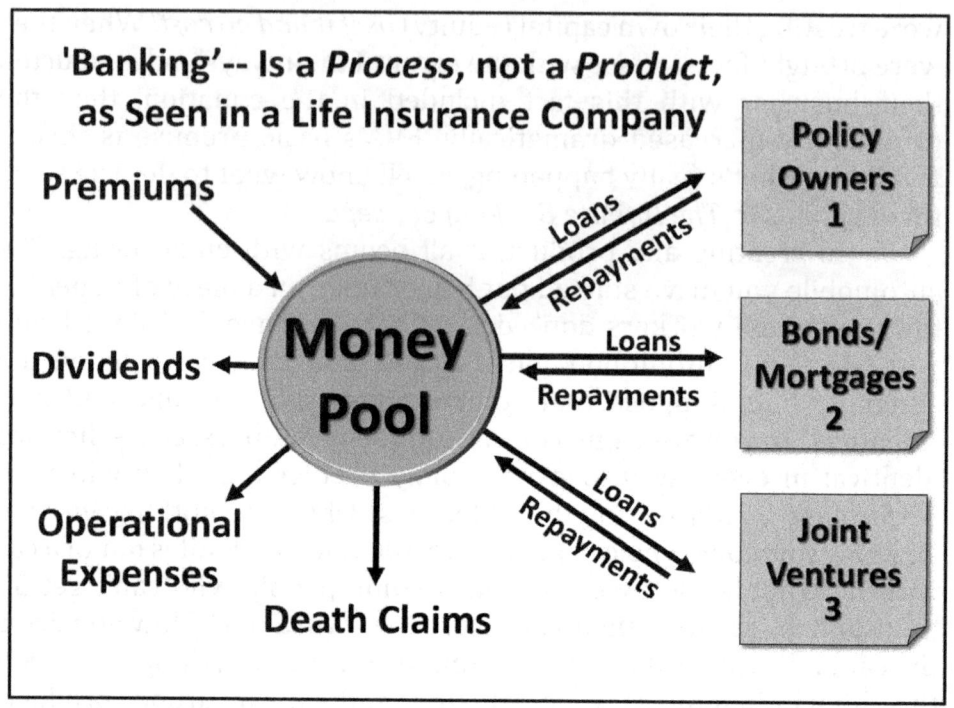

To make the plan work the Owner must make payments into it and the Company (the hired-help) *must put the money to work* in order to produce the benefits that are promised. Those with the investment responsibility will do so in a number of ways, putting it into financial instruments that are fairly conservative, e.g. bonds, mortgages, etc.

But, upon reading the contract (the policy) you will find it plainly stated that the *Owner outranks every potential borrower in access to the money that must be lent!* And what he can borrow is 100% of his equity in the contract (the amount that the company can lend at any one time). If this is true—which it is—then what this amounts to is *absolute control* over the investment function of the company as it relates to the owner's policy. In essence, money can be lent to the other places *only if the owner of the policy* does not exercise his option to use the money (and pay interest) instead.

As a result of the foregoing, there is an ever-increasing pool of money. From time to time an insured person dies. It doesn't happen very often—but when it does, the company pays the beneficiary from the pool of money and the cost of doing so is allocated among the policy owners on an equitable basis.

The "hired help," the administrators, must be paid for their work, too. You can't run a business without "hired help." Just try to do it and see what happens. Your competitors who know better will run you out of business. This cost is pro-rated among the policy owners, too.

At the end of the year the directors who actually run the company call the accountants in and, in essence, ask them, "How did we do this year on John Doe's policy in comparison with the assumptions made by the actuaries and the rate-makers in designing it?"

We must digress at this point and remember that an actuary is a kind of engineer and that all engineers "overbuild" everything they design. Furthermore, the policy is engineered to become more efficient every year, no matter what happens (that is, if the Owner does what is called for in premium paying, loan repayments plus interest thereon that are at least equal to or better than the general investment portfolio of the company). That is because the cash value is *guaranteed* to ultimately reach the face amount of the policy by the endowment age (which used to be 100 years but occurs at age 121 on newer policies). There is an ever-decreasing "net amount at risk" for the company.

In designing the life insurance policy the rate-makers have taken into consideration the advice of the actuaries that their assumptions are *not set in concrete.* They include the interest earnings on the premiums paid by policy owners, the death claims expected during a time frame, and the expected cost of administration. Over a long period of time the actuaries can be pretty accurate, but from time to time the results can be better or worse than predicted. There are variations in interest earnings, death claims, and expenses of operations and these factors affect the dividend scale declared for the coming year.

The Whole Life Insurance Dividend

$1.00 - Actuarial Projected Cost of Insurance

$1.10 - Statutory Collected Premium
 -.80 - Actual Cost of Insurance
  .30 - Divisible Surplus
 -.025 - Contingency Fund
  .275 - Dividend

Premium → Money Pool → Dividend

You can safely say that the real results will *never* exactly match the illustration provided at the beginning of the life of a policy. But, once a dividend is declared, it can't be taken back. If you elect to use your dividend to buy additional insurance—thus boosting the cash value and death benefit—those increments in your policy can't go down in future years, even if the life insurance company does poorly.

A significant period of *lower* than expected earnings of interest, or a period of *more* than expected death claims and/or administrative expenses can result in a "downer" for the company. When this happens in a regular corporation it is the function of the stockholders to "take up the slack." But, in this case, the rate-makers are reminded that *"we don't have any stockholders!"* So, the rate-makers are cautioned by the actuaries that "if we calculate that it would require $1.00 per year for a given plan, don't collect $1.00—

collect $1.10." This *extra* .10 is the *capital* that makes the whole system viable.

Now back to our scene on John Doe's policy. He has had it for a few years and the Directors have asked the accountants, "How did we do on John Doe's policy this year?" The accountants report that they had collected $1.10 but after calculating all the aforementioned factors they found that it took only 80 cents to deliver that promised death benefit in the future. This means the directors can make a decision with 30 cents. If they are "half-way" smart (and most of them are) they will take into consideration that they need to put a part of this into a *contingency fund* to prepare for unexpected future risks. So, they put .025 into the *contingency fund* and distribute .275 and call it a "dividend." Most people have the impression that this is a taxable event. This is not so. Remember that the modern income tax has only been with us since 1913 (the U.S. got along very well without it prior to that time; there were *surpluses* in the federal budget) and life insurance has been around for over 200 years. The word *dividend* was used by the insurance industry to describe this dispersal and it stuck with us, but the correct classification is a *return of premium* (or a return of capital), which is not a taxable event (under certain circumstances). If the owner uses the dividend to purchase Additional Paid-Up Insurance (no cost for acquisition, sales commissions, etc.) the result is an ever-increasing tax-deferred accumulation of cash values that support an ever-increasing death benefit. And there are no government bureaucrats looking over your shoulder telling you what you can and cannot do. The result is limited only by the imagination of the policy owner.

(Note, we are speaking in broad strokes here to get the basics across to a newcomer. There are specific rules governing the tax treatment of life insurance policies. You should consult with a financial professional who has graduated from our program to receive information tailored to your circumstances: www.InfiniteBanking.org/Finder.)

By the way, these dividends can get pretty significant over a long period of time. For example, Nelson Nash bought a policy from a major insurance company in 1959 and the annual dividend as of this writing is more than *ten times* the annual premium. The recent annual dividend payments would have been much larger had Nash not used the annual dividend to *reduce premiums* for the first 15 years of the policy. These things are just not adequately explained by typical life insurance sales folks because of the limited understanding of their home office folks who teach them. A pity!

The Problem and Solution: A Simple Example

Now let us return to our hypothetical young man who typifies the "average American" and exemplifies the problem. Remember that he is paying more than 35% of every dollar of after-tax income to interest charges. It should be obvious that his *need for finance* is much greater than his *need for life insurance protection.* If he would solve for the need for finance through dividend-paying Whole Life insurance, he would *automatically* have much more life insurance (i.e. death benefit coverage) *and recover all the interest he is now paying to someone else.* But this almost never occurs because of the mental block implanted by financial geniuses that "life insurance is a poor place to store money." What a limited outlook of just what is going on in the banking world! Again we remind you, if you know what's really happening, you'll know what to do.

Consider the way the typical household deals with the twin problems of obtaining death benefit coverage and obtaining the services of an automobile. First, the young man puts, say, $50 per month into term life insurance premiums and feels that he is "insurance poor." (He is worth more dead than alive, etc.)

Second, our young man goes down to a car dealer and buys an automobile, paying for it with a loan from a bank or finance company. Remember that there is only *one pool of money* out there in the world. The fact that many organizations and individuals are managing a portion of the pool is incidental. But, it can be even more specific when it comes to automobile loans: if one inspects the list of investments from major life insurance companies you will see *finance companies* as a place where they have loaned blocks of money. The finance company simply buys blocks of money, adds a fee to it for their service, and loans it to consumers who buy cars. So, our hypothetical man pays, say, $260 per month for a minimum of 48 months for his $10,550 car loan. He does this throughout life because that's the way all his peers are doing it.

If he would take time out, and stand back far enough to get some perspective, our young man might notice that he is paying $50 per month into a pool of money (the life insurance policy) and paying $260 per month to an intermediary (the finance company that deducts a fee and lives *well* off the activity) which passes the residual sum back to the *same pool* of money! Furthermore, he complains about the premium he pays but thinks nothing of the much larger amount he pays the automobile finance company! Strange, isn't it?

In the above example, our man is paying a total of $310 to the pool: $50 directly and $260 indirectly. If he could muster up the courage to pay the $310 *directly to the life insurance company* in the form of premiums (on a Whole Life policy, rather than a term policy) for around four years, he could now take out a policy loan and pay cash for the automobile!

In such a scenario he would have capitalized a banking system!

Here comes the important part again, so pay close attention! If this is the approach our man pursues, the life insurance agent needs to make him *vividly* aware that he must *pay the loan back at an interest rate that is at least equivalent to the going interest rate of an automobile finance company*—not what the "policy loan interest rate" is, as specified in the life insurance contract. In this case it should be at least $260 per month. If the policyholder does this, then he will effectively *make* what the finance company would otherwise make and do it all on a tax-free basis. If the agent is really good, and understands the principles of banking, he will encourage the policyholder to pay $275 per month because the "extra" dollars will go to his policy to *increase the capital* that can be lent to other parties.[i]

If the policyholder objects that, "it's my own money and I am not going to pay any interest at all"—or maybe, "I'm only going to pay 2.9% as seen in television commercials"—then the agent must remind him *that he is not borrowing "his money."* He is borrowing money from the insurance company's portfolio and putting up his cash value as collateral. (Hence, this is the safest loan that the life insurance company can make!) Furthermore, remember the lessons of EVA: Investing money always carries a "cost of capital," even if it's "your own money." If you are going to act like a banker, you must not behave as if money borrowed against your life insurance policy is "free."

Looking At A Life Insurance Policy Over A Long Period of Time

How you *think* is everything! Most people don't think long range.

After ten years of working as a Consulting Forester, working in the life insurance industry as an agent for 35 years, and lecturing on the subject of life insurance for an additional 17 years, plus purchasing lots of life policies beginning when he was age 13, it became evident to Nelson Nash that people just don't look at the performance of a dividend-paying Whole Life policy over *a long enough period of time.* They only consider the results during the first few years—say, ten years at the longest. Such a policy is engineered to get better, every day, as long as the policy is in force. The earlier one starts, the longer one continues, the better the policy gets.

Since Nash was educated as a forester, he tends to think about things over a much longer period of time, something like 70 years. "Plan as if you are going to live forever, but live as if you are going to die today," sounds like a good idea.

Take a look at the results of the last 20 years of a policy Nash bought from State Farm Life in 1959 to adjust your own perspective. Nash bought this policy from his brother, a State Farm Agent, while Nash was a forester in North Carolina.

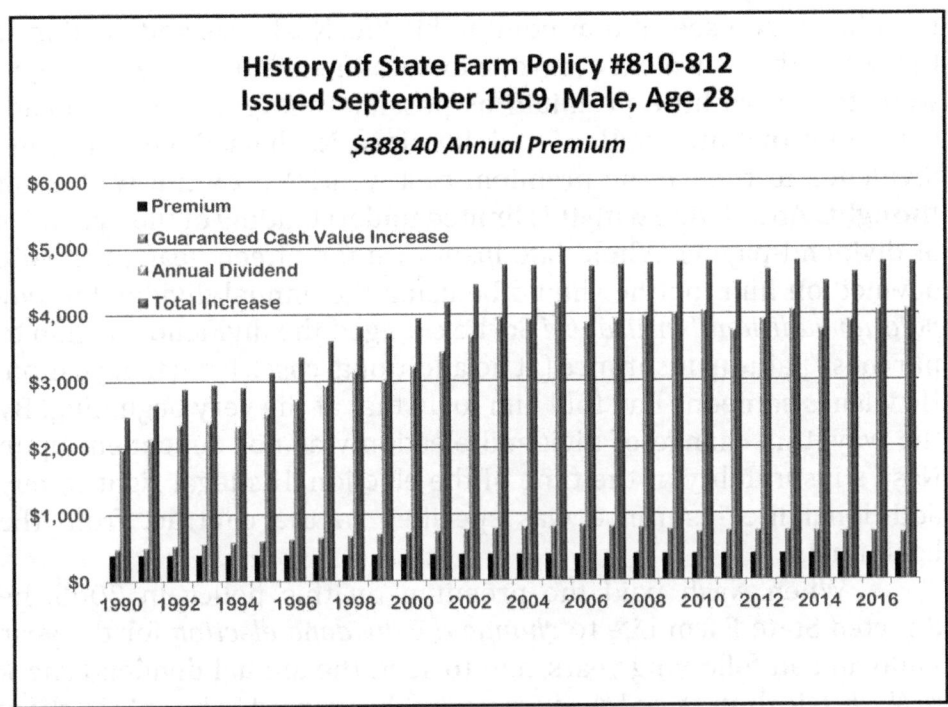

At the time of this writing, the policy is 58 years old. That's about one-fourth of the time that Whole Life insurance has been in existence. The bars on the graph represent the **actual performance** on a *year-to-year* basis. That is, you are not looking at *cumulative* results at any one point on the graph. For instance, in 1990 Nash paid $388.40 premium. The Guaranteed Cash Value *increase*, that year, was $500.00. The dividend, that year, was $2,000.00. The *total increase* in cash value was $2,500.00. The increases for each of the following years were *added to the values of the preceding years.*

Now, let's fast-forward and look at the year 2005. Notice that the Guaranteed Cash Value increased $800.00 and the dividend was $4,200.00 resulting in a $5,000.00 total increase that year. Of course, all that Nash paid that year was $388.40.

Notice that the dividend now is *ten times the premium*. It would have been *twelve times* the premium had Nash not used dividends for the first fifteen years of the policy to reduce the premiums! You see, at that point in his life, Nash was still looking at the policy the way most everyone looks at life insurance, where "you want to pay as little premium as possible and get as much death benefit for that little outlay," and therefore, Nash used the increasing dividends to reduce the premium each year. **That's the way Nash thought!** After living with this limited understanding of the dynamics of dividend-paying Whole Life insurance for fifteen years, it finally dawned on him that he should be using the annual dividend to *buy paid-up additional insurance!* So, he changed the dividend election to purchase paid-up insurance (at no additional cost), from that year on. He wishes someone had told him to do that at the very beginning! By the way, this change of dividend election was not dependent upon Nash's insurability at the time of the election. His legal right to buy additional life insurance was specified in the contract from the beginning.

When Nash paid the premium on this policy in 2005, he directed State Farm Life to *change the dividend election* for the year 2006 and all following years, and to send the annual dividend *check to Nash*. (He didn't need the income, but he wanted to be able to show the dividend check to those non-believers.)

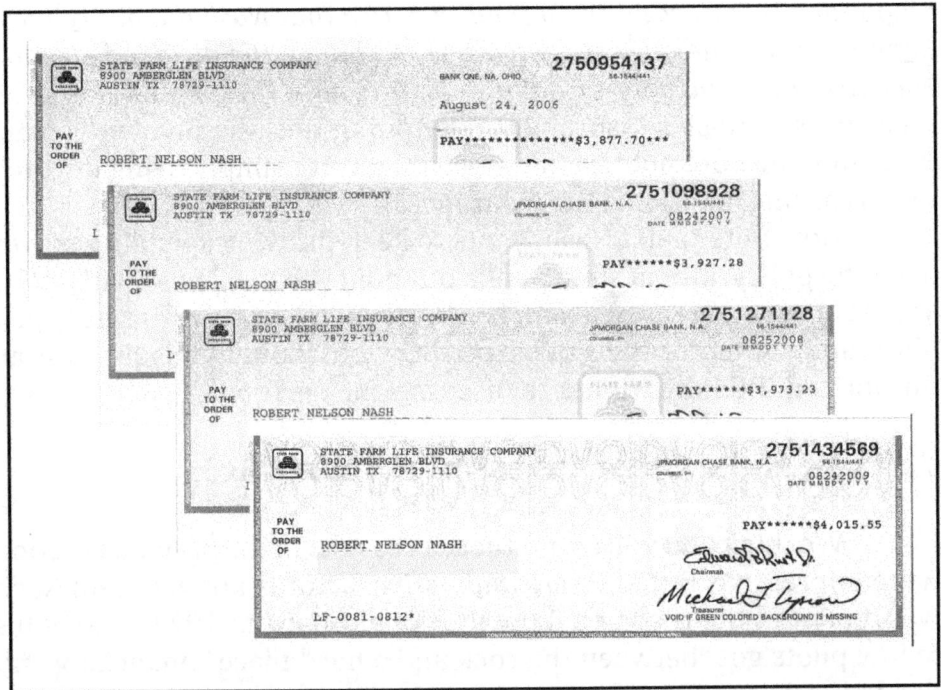

The check for 2006 was $3,877.70, for 2007 it was $3,927.28, for 2008 it was $3,973, for 2009 it was $4,015.

So, let's do some basic arithmetic: Take the annual premium ($388.00) per year and multiply by the number of years the policy had been in force at that point in time (52). That is Nash's *gross outlay*. Now, subtract the value of the dividends he used to reduce premiums the first fifteen years. We have now isolated Nash's *net cost of the policy to date (his "cost basis" for the policy)*.

These dividend checks were all income-tax-free because they were less than what Nash had paid into the policy over the years up to that point. However, in July of 2010, Nash got a letter from State Farm requesting that he furnish his Social Security Number to make sure their records were correct, *because by that point Nash had recovered all the cost basis of the policy*. Therefore, all the dividend checks in the future would be *taxable*, since they would represent money above and beyond what Nash had "put into" the policy. Nash responded by *directing them (please notice that Nash did not <u>request them</u> to do so—he gave them orders) to change the dividend election back to purchasing paid-up additional insurance* (again, this was done regardless of Nash's insurability). By doing this, the dividends from that point on were not taxable, since they were simply being devoted to purchasing additional life insurance.

Now note that if Nash wants to keep drawing spending power from the policy, he can simply take out policy loans. These will *not* be a taxable event, because a loan is not income. Again, we are here just illustrating some of the power of IBC; you should consult with an Authorized IBC Practitioner to discuss your personal situation.

You Can Make Other Investments With IBC

We think you will admit that the results in the previous section were impressive. But, the *very impressive* factor is not yet seen! Nash was a pilot in the Alabama Army National Guard in 1971. One of his fellow pilots got "between the rock and a hard place" financially and needed to raise some money.

He knew Nash was educated as a Forester and might be interested in buying the 100 acres of timberland he owned in northwest Alabama. He said, "I'll sell it to you for $50.00 per acre, and I will finance it for you for ten years." Nash knew that was a good deal and took it, and made monthly payments to him. This was not a speculative venture; it was property that Nash knew something about. (Remember, he was educated as a Forester and worked in that field for ten years.)

About 18 months later, the man called Nash again and requested that they get together to talk. He said, "I underestimated my need for cash. If you will just pay off the debt on that land now, I will discount it 25 cents on the dollar." Nash knew that was a good deal so replied, "Stand real still—I'll be right back." Nash went directly to the regional State Farm office and said, "Get me a $3,500 policy loan quickly before this young man changes his mind!" In less than an hour, Nash had a check in his hand.

Bottom line: Nash had less than $38 per acre invested in that land. In 1985, he sold that land for $500 per acre, and he had financed it for 10 years at 15% interest! With that income, Nash paid back the policy loan (which he originally gave to the man) and then bought more life insurance. All those premiums become cost basis in the new policy and Nash will get it back, tax free, when he decides to draw "passive income" (dividends) from it.

During the following years, Nash made two more investments from policy loans on this policy. The results were not quite as good, but still they were highly profitable. These facts are not seen as you look at the earlier graph showing the performance of the State Farm policy. You have to add these results to what is shown on the graph to understand the total power of dividend-paying Whole Life insurance. This is what "BUILDING YOUR WAREHOUSE OF WEALTH" is all about. You have almost immediate access to money to take advantage of opportunities that will surely appear. In fact, if you have a readily available pool of cash, opportunities will "track you down."

If you elect to have the annual dividend buy additional paid-up insurance (which cannot be denied due to your health status), what you have is an ever-compounding increase in cash value with no tax consequences, so long as you have handled your affairs properly.

IBC Works For Business Investments, Too

Shortly before Nash bought the State Farm policy from his brother, he was called upon by a representative of a financial services company (which shall remain nameless) who showed him a "mountain wave graph of lies" about how good Nash would have done in the stock market if he had put $10,000 into it twenty years earlier.

"Do you have $10,000 to put into such a plan today?" he asked. "No," Nash replied. The man responded, "Don't worry about it. We have an accumulation plan in which you can put $50 per month ($600 per year) and, *in time*, it will become $10,000. At that time we can put it into one of our mutual funds and you will be set for life!" Nash indulged. The agent made Nash initial the point on his projection at which Nash's outlay would equal its value. It was *eight years!*

So, Nash was paying $600 per year in that plan and $388.40 to the State Farm policy. That's $1,000 per year—10% of Nash's annual income at the time. Remember, it was Nash's next older brother that sold him the SF policy. He knew about the $600 that Nash was paying into the other plan. What if brother had suggested that Nash pay the entire $1,000 into the SF policy? Then, the dividend check that Nash is now receiving would be more than $10,000 per year! And, Nash would have had more money in the interim years to take advantage of investments that would have come along. If, in this scenario, Nash had bought paid-up additional insurance with the dividends for *all the years* of this policy, then the dividend would have been $12,000 per year!

Furthermore, brother knew that Nash was running heavy equipment (Caterpillar tractors) to clear land for tree growing purposes in his business. Nash was paying a finance company $1,500 per month on heavy equipment.

That's $18,000 per year! Where did the finance company get the money to lend Nash? From insurance companies! Remember, finance companies buy "blocks" of money from insurance companies, fragment those blocks and sell the money to consumers, who agree to pay back the finance company monthly over a period of time—adding a higher interest rate, of course.

Brother should have taught Nash to pay $18,000 per year in life insurance premiums to accumulate a pool of capital from which, eventually, Nash could finance *all* his forestry equipment. There was no way Nash could do that *immediately* since his income was $10,000 per year. But, brother could have sold Nash, say, four times the amount that he did, and in a few years Nash could have been rid of one of those tractor payments forever.

Nash could have been earning what the outside finance company was making off of him, with advantageous tax treatment, for the balance of his life. Once a person gets past the point of financing one item in his scenario, he can accelerate the process very quickly. In about 15 years, a businessperson can be **totally self-sufficient**.

Question: Why didn't his brother teach Nelson these things? Answer: He didn't know. Question: Why didn't he know? Answer: State Farm Life didn't teach him!

Well, why didn't they teach him? All the qualities of dividend-paying Whole Life insurance that Infinite Banking Concepts teaches have been there for 200 years! All because of how they **thought!**

Nash's brother died on the first day of January 1981 at age 52. As of this writing, Nelson is 86, so, in the not too distant future, the two brothers will be reunited. Both men were strong Christians. This earthly existence is simply "training camp for the eternal."

Nash assures us that when they get over the pleasantries of meeting again, then he is going to ask his brother: "Why didn't you sell me much more life insurance than you did?"

"What About Inflation?"

One more point needs addressing. Many "financial geniuses" say that inflation will "eat your Whole Life insurance alive." So let's examine the facts. When Nash bought his policy the initial death benefit was $20,000. At of this writing it is $130,000. That's 6.5 times the initial amount! What if, during those first 15 years of the policy, Nash had used the increasing dividends to buy paid up additional insurance? Then the current death benefit would be over $150,000! That would be 7.5 times the initial death benefit!

You must consider this as well: Nash has been paying premiums annually that have been decreasing in value. The dollar that Nash recently paid has only one-fifth the power of the dollar he paid in 1959—yet the death benefit has gone up faster than general price inflation.

Conclusion

In the interest of brevity, we must conclude this introduction to Nelson Nash's revolutionary concept. For a fuller treatment, you must read *Becoming Your Own Banker*.

We leave you with Nash's five rules for success with IBC:

> # FIVE SIMPLE RULES TO IBC
> ....
>
> * THINK LONG RANGE
>
> * BE GENEROUS IN CAPITALIZING YOUR SYSTEM
>
> * DON'T STEAL FROM YOUR SYSTEM
>
> * DON'T DO BUSINESS WITH BANKS
>
> * RETHINK YOUR THINKING

---

[i] To avoid confusion: If someone implements IBC and uses a policy loan in order to buy a car without needing an outside finance company, then Nelson Nash typically recommends that the person "makes the same monthly car payment" (at least) back into the personal banking system. So for example, if the conventional method of auto financing would have implied a $260 monthly car payment, then the person using IBC should still devote that much out of general household cashflow into the IBC policy. Even better, Nash recommends devoting more, say, $275 per month. Now in practice, this aggressive payment schedule will knock out the actual policy loan (used to buy the car originally) ahead of time. In that case, the additional "car payments" would be used to buy more paid-up life insurance.

Chapter 5

How Does This Work?

The Economics of IBC

So far in this book, we've diagnosed *the economic problem* facing business owners and households, in which they use State-issued fiat money coupled with a rigged commercial and investment banking system. We then presented *the solution* of "becoming your own banker" through the use of a properly designed, dividend-paying Whole Life insurance policy.

We recognize that some of our claims may have seemed too good to be true. The public has been subject to so many lies in this arena—from government officials, academic intellectuals, and unscrupulous salesmen—that IBC might sound like just another gimmick.

To reassure skeptical readers, and to solidify the understanding of those who are already convinced, this chapter explains the mechanics of IBC from an economics perspective. Specifically, we respond to some of the common objections and questions we've encountered over the years.

➔ **QUESTION #1:** "If this is about 'becoming your own banker,' why do you guys keep talking about life insurance?"

ANSWER: Remember that IBC stands for the Infinite Banking *Concept*. At its deepest level, IBC is about transforming the way you *think* about money, and how it flows into and out of your possession.

Action starts in the mind, but it results in observable behavior. When someone uses a *means* to achieve an *end*, there is both a subjective and an objective component. Likewise, even though IBC is an abstract *process*, it must be implemented on a tangible *platform*. Specifically, a properly designed, dividend-paying Whole Life insurance policy is the ideal *vehicle* through which you "become your own banker."

There is nothing intrinsic to life insurance to connect it to IBC. It's simply the case that there is no better way of implementing IBC than through the use of a life insurance policy of the structure we have been describing. (By the end of this chapter, you will have a much better idea of the *specifics* of why this is the case.)

In order to practice IBC as Nelson Nash envisioned, it is necessary to make large premium payments to build up the cash surrender value of a life insurance policy, so that large policy loans will be available when needed. It is impossible to make the case for this financial lifestyle to someone who doesn't understand how or why the life insurance company makes loans to policyholders. (Imagine trying to teach someone how to buy things with money, who didn't understand what a wallet or a purse was.)

In order to teach the public the virtues of "becoming your own banker," we also have to teach the basics of Whole Life insurance.

➔ **QUESTION #2:** "What if I'm uninsurable? Can I still practice IBC?"

ANSWER: Yes! Even if you personally are uninsurable, you can still practice IBC by taking out appropriately designed Whole Life insurance policies on anyone in whom you have an insurable interest. This could be your spouse, children, grandchildren, or even business partners.

It's important to reiterate that the *owner* of the life insurance contract—also known as the *policyholder*—doesn't need to be the same person who is the *insured*. For example, if Jim Smith learns about IBC but he personally has a serious heart condition, he can still take out a policy on (say) his daughter, Mary. In this case, Jim can pay the premiums to keep Mary's policy in force, and Jim can take out policy loans against the accumulating cash surrender value in Mary's policy. If he wants, down the road Jim can transfer ownership and control of this particular policy to Mary when she is an adult (after Jim has "banked" with it for two decades).

Always keep in mind that we are ultimately implementing IBC through the use of *life insurance* policies. As such, you must have an insurable interest in a person if you wish to take out a policy on his or her life, and furthermore the size of the policy must bear some relationship to the economic magnitude of this interest. For example, two business partners who jointly run a $10 million business might take out multimillion-dollar life insurance policies on each other, because if one of them were to suddenly die, that would have tremendous financial consequences for the other.

In contrast, if two partners jointly run a hot dog stand, they would not be able to take out such large policies on each other. The principle here is that the function of the death benefit is to *compensate the named beneficiary* in the event of death. Consider an analogy with car insurance: It makes sense that the owner of a new Ferrari could have an auto policy that would indemnify him with $300,000 in the event of a crash, whereas the owner of a Honda Civic couldn't get such a large auto policy, even if he were willing to pay the same premiums. The principle of "insurable interest" ensures that the insurance companies are compensating people for losses, rather than letting them speculate on rare events. (Among other considerations, the insurance companies don't want people having an incentive to crash their Honda Civic or to have their hot dog partner killed!)

Two final points in our necessarily brief treatment of this topic: First, if you take out a life insurance policy on someone in whom you have an insurable interest, that policy stays in force (so long as you pay the contractual premiums) even if the insurable interest goes away. Second, there are many nuances with taking out policies on other people. We are simply answering the basic question that yes, you can still practice IBC in your personal or business life, even if you personally have a medical condition that makes you uninsurable.

➔**QUESTION #3: "Doesn't everybody know that Whole Life is a terrible investment? All the investment experts say you should 'buy term and invest the difference.'"**

ANSWER: It's true, investment gurus such as Dave Ramsey and Suze Orman say that you're a sucker if you buy into a Whole Life (or other permanent) life insurance policy. They use statistics about stock market performance to apparently "prove" that you do much better following the strategy of "buy term and invest the difference." Specifically, they will take a particular life insurance goal—such as a death benefit coverage of $500,000—and figure out how much it would take a certain person (such as a 25-year-old male in good health) to get a cash-value life insurance policy, and compare that to the price of, say, a 20-year term policy with the same $500,000 in death benefit coverage. Naturally, the premium on the cash-value policy will be much higher than the premium for the term policy. So Dave Ramsey et al. advise their listeners to opt for "the same" death benefit coverage with the cheaper term policy, and then "invest the difference" (meaning how much you save in the premium outlay) into a diversified mutual fund tied to the stock market. Using historical experience from mutual fund performance, the gurus seem to demonstrate that over time, the value of the mutual fund will grow faster than the cash available in the permanent insurance policy. Since the death benefit coverage (by construction) is the same, and since the available cash in the mutual fund is more than the cash in the permanent life insurance policy, it seems like only a fool would put his money into one of these "overfunded" life policies.

There are so many things wrong with this analysis that it's hard to know where to begin.[i] Yet before we dive in, let us be clear: We are *not* criticizing the use of term life insurance. For many situations, a term policy makes perfect sense. (Indeed, one of the sophisticated approaches to designing a large IBC policy involves the use of a "term rider" appended to a Whole Life chassis.) For example, a young couple with several children should have a large life insurance policy on the primary breadwinner, so that the family is not devastated financially in case of premature death. In order to get adequate death benefit coverage, the couple will probably only be able to afford a term policy, which will last through the vulnerable period as the family builds up assets, sends the kids through school, sees the breadwinner's income rise, etc. Proponents of IBC have no problem with people using term policies in certain situations.

What we *are* saying is that Dave Ramsey and the other glib critics are wrong when they argue that people should *only* buy term life insurance. No, there are pros and cons associated with the different types of insurance policies, and Ramsey et al. are comparing them with a tilted scale. The typical demonstration of the superiority of "buy term and invest the difference" only seems to work because it compares apples to oranges.

First of all, when you buy a Whole Life policy with a given death benefit, you are entitled to that coverage (so long as you keep paying the premium) for your *whole life*—that's where the name comes from. In contrast, if you take out (say) a 20-year term policy, then at the end of 20 years, you lose the ability to keep the coverage in force with the same level premium. You will have to go again into the market to obtain a new policy, and since you're older, the premium will be much higher or—if you have developed a serious medical condition—you might be uninsurable altogether.

Here's a fun experiment to understand just how significant this fact is. Go to an online insurance quote generator to see what the cost would be for, say, a 25-year-old nonsmoking male in good health, to get $500,000 in death benefit coverage for life insurance policies with terms of 10, 20, and 30 years. You will see that the level premium quoted for the 10-year term policy is quite cheap, but that the premium for the 20-year policy is a bit higher and for the 30-year policy is higher still. Now ask yourself: Why is this the case? The reason, of course, is that the older you get, the more likely you are to die. When a healthy 25-year-old takes out a 10-year term policy, he is probably going to make those premium payments and never take a cent from the insurance company. Therefore the insurance company can afford to offer him coverage at a surprisingly low monthly price. However, if that same 25-year-old takes out a 30-year term policy, then near the end of the period he'll be in his fifties when it's much more likely that he could die, in which case the insurance company has to mail out that $500,000 check. Consequently, if the insurance company is going to charge the same level premium for the entire length of the policy, that number has to be a lot higher than it was for the 10-year policy.

So far, so good. Now consider what it means if our hypothetical 25-year-old instead takes out a Whole Life policy. In this case, the man can keep his policy in force *forever*, so long as he pays the premium (which is locked in and never goes up, even if the man develops a medical condition). Modern policies of this type are designed to "endow" at age 121, meaning that if the person lives that long, then the insurance company pays out the face value "death benefit." Therefore, we can think of a Whole Life policy as effectively being a *96-year* term policy! (When the 25-year-old takes out such a policy, 96 years pass before he turns 121.) Since you saw how the premiums on regular term policies rapidly rise, going from 10- to 20- to 30-year term structures, you can appreciate why an effective 96-year term policy would have such a relatively high premium. This doesn't indicate corruption or shoddiness, it indicates how much *value* the policyholder is obtaining by opening up a Whole Life policy.

So far we've seen that when Dave Ramsey or the other gurus argue that their approach provides the "same death benefit coverage," they are incorrect, because at the end of the term period, the individual will either have to pay significantly higher premiums on a new term policy, or the individual will simply drop coverage altogether.[ii] This is why it's completely illegitimate to look at the value of a mutual fund in (say) Year 23 of the strategy and compare it to the cash value of the permanent life insurance policy, because if the individual were to die at this point, the "buy term and invest the difference" strategy would mean *no death benefit* check. Ramsey et al. think they have neatly separated the death benefit and investment vehicle aspects, but they haven't, since "buy term and invest the difference" only provides death benefit coverage for the duration of the initial term policy, while the permanent life policy provides death benefit coverage for the entire lifespan.

Yet there is another, subtler problem with the comparison. A standard IBC policy will be designed in such a way that the dividends it generates *and* a significant portion of the out-of-pocket outlays (what we can call the premium[iii]) are channeled into buying additional insurance as the policy ages. So even if we start out (by assumption) with a policy that has $500,000 in face-value death benefit coverage, as the years pass the death benefit will increase. In contrast, the standard term policy that Dave Ramsey would have you buy, will stay put with the original death benefit coverage. So even if we focus just on the period of the original term policy, as the years pass, the amount of protection you have using the IBC approach continues to grow while the "buy term and invest the difference" level of protection stays constant.

Finally, it is completely illegitimate to compare the "expected" value of a mutual fund tied to the stock market, with the cash values of an IBC-type policy. Yes, the "internal rate of return" in the former is higher than in the latter. But this overlooks the *risk* of the two types of assets. A mutual fund that tracks, say, the S&P 500 index can crash—just look at what happened in 2008 and 2009. In contrast, the cash values in a life insurance policy can *never* go down, and they also have built-in guaranteed rates of growth. It's true, with these guarantees in place, the life insurance policy can only promise a much more modest expected rate of growth, compared to the volatile stock market. For investors who want to chase higher yields with the risk of loss, exposure to the stock market might make sense. But to merely look at the historical rate of return in an equity-based mutual fund, and compare it to the internal rate of return on life insurance, as if that were the *only* criterion, is obviously foolish. One might just as well "prove" that stocks are better to own than bonds, or that a leveraged hedge fund is obviously a better investment than one without leverage.

As these considerations have shown, the glib "buy term and invest the difference" demonstrations are based on incomplete analysis and faulty comparisons. There are certain situations in which a term life insurance policy makes perfect sense, but there other scenarios in which a Whole Life policy is more appropriate. There's nothing irrational or foolish about buying a standard Whole Life policy, and its benefits only increase when you learn how to use it as a vehicle for IBC.

➔ **QUESTION #4: "I heard that those sneaky life insurance companies keep your cash values when you die—your beneficiary only gets the death benefit."**

ANSWER: Because typical life insurance "illustrations"—meaning tables that project the performance of the policy over time—show columns for both the "Cash Surrender Value" and "Death Benefit" available each year in the future, some members of the public who are new to this topic can understandably become confused. So to be crystal clear: While the insured is *alive*, the policyholder can only take out policy loans (or surrender the policy) up to the amount of the available cash. When the insured *dies* (or reaches the age at which the policy completes, such as 121 years old), then the life insurance company pays out the *death benefit* but *only* the death benefit. However, as we'll explain, there is nothing devious about this procedure; once we understand what the cash surrender value *is*, it should be obvious that the beneficiaries of a policy would only get the death benefit, and nothing else on top of that.

For those readers who want a technical definition, you can think of the *cash surrender value* as the (present-discounted value of the actuarially expected) death benefit payment minus the future flow of remaining premium payments. For example, consider a 35-year-old who takes out a Whole Life policy that provides a $1 million death benefit and requires level annual premium payments of $10,000. (Note that we are picking round numbers for the example; these are not actual price quotes from the market.) At the moment the policy is issued, it has a cash surrender value of $0. This is because the insurance company's actuaries and market strategists reckon the flow of expected premium payments—taking into account the uncertain timing of death, as well as the "time value" of money—from this 35-year-old is of comparable value to the liability of the looming death benefit payment that he will eventually be paid (if he keeps the policy in force). With each year that passes, however, the in-force policy becomes a greater and greater liability to the life insurance company. This is because the death benefit payout of $1 million is now one year closer (and so its value in present-dollar terms goes up), while there is one fewer premium payment of $10,000 that will come in from the policyholder. Thus, over time, the amount the life insurance company would be willing to pay the policyholder to *walk away* from the policy—and thus release the company from its obligation to pay out $1 million upon death—goes up, year after year. In other words, the amount of cash that the life insurance company would be willing to pay upon the *surrender* of the policy, steadily rises year after year. This is a somewhat technical way of understanding what the "cash surrender value" is, and why it rises over time.[iv]

For those readers wanting a more intuitive explanation, think of it like this: When the life insurance company enters a binding contract with a policyholder, they each take on certain obligations. The policyholder promises to pay a string of premiums while still alive, and the insurance company promises to pay a large sum upon death. In order to fulfill its side of the deal, the insurance company must take those incoming premium payments and "put them to work" by buying assets that hopefully generate a return. If the actuaries and other experts have done their jobs, then the insurance company will oversee a portfolio of financial assets that will be able to pay out the death benefits as the claims occur. If, at any point in this business, one of the outstanding policyholders is willing to cancel the policy *before* the insured party actually dies, then the insurance company would be willing and able to make a lump-sum payment in order to get the policyholder to walk away. The longer the policy has been in force, the more premium payments its owner has paid in, and the longer they've been "at work" earning income for the insurance company. This is why the company can afford to make a bigger surrender payment to the policyholder, the more mature the policy has become.

To summarize: The cash surrender value is a "spot payment" that is necessarily *smaller* than the death benefit. It is what the insurance company will pay in order to remove a ticking time bomb from the Liabilities side of its balance sheet. However, if the insured person happens to die while the policy is still in force, then *of course* the life insurance company will only pay the death benefit to the named beneficiary. To insist on payment of the death benefit *and* "the cash value" wouldn't make any sense; it misunderstands what the cash surrender value *is*.

To see how nonsensical it would be to ask for the cash value on top of the death benefit, consider this analogy: Suppose a man takes out a 30-year mortgage to buy a $300,000 home, where he put 20% down. In the beginning, the man's CPA tells him that he has $60,000 of equity in the house, and an outstanding mortgage balance of $240,000. With each monthly payment, the outstanding principal on the mortgage shrinks, while the market price of the house gently rises over time. Fifteen years into the deal, the man checks in with his CPA, who informs him that the market price of the house is $400,000, while the principal of the mortgage is now only $150,000. At this point, the CPA tells him, the man has about $250,000 in equity in the house—much more than the $60,000 at the time of purchase. Finally, after the 360th monthly payment, the mortgage is finally cleared. The bank teller congratulates the man and hands over the deed to the house. The man then asks the bank teller for a check for $500,000, which is how much the house is now worth on the market. The bank teller is confused. The man explains, "Yes, you gave me the deed to the house, but I *also* want my equity, which is now $500,000 as my accountant informs me. I hope you aren't trying to be sneaky by keeping my equity and only handing over the deed!"

In this silly story, it is clear that the bank did nothing deceptive or fraudulent. The "equity" the man was building in the house was the market value minus the remaining mortgage balance, which was a lien against the asset. So yes, the passage of time tended to make the market value of the house rise, and it made the outstanding balance on the loan fall (with each monthly payment), so that the net equity kept rising over time. But it would be nonsense to expect the bank to pay for the equity in the house, beyond the simple fact of handing over the deed to the underlying asset.

Likewise, when it comes to Whole Life insurance, the passage of time brings the death benefit closer, and it reduces the number of premium payments the policyholder must pay, in order to receive that (future) payout. So the difference between the two—which we can think of as the "equity" being built up in the policy—grows over time; this is what drives the cash surrender value. But the fundamental, underlying asset is the death benefit payout; the cash surrender value is just the *anticipation* of that future event, discounted into a fewer number of present-dollars. However, *when* death actually occurs and the life insurance company hands over the full death benefit, it would be nonsense to expect a separate payment for the "cash value" in the policy. In an accounting sense, the "cash value" of the policy *is* exactly equal to the death benefit, once the insured person has died—just like the equity you have in your house is exactly equal to its market value, once you've paid off the mortgage.

In summary: Yes, it is true that the life insurance company only pays out the death benefit, and not the cash surrender value, in the event of death. However, this simply reflects the nature of what the cash surrender value *is*.

➔**QUESTION #5: "IBC is really just a way to build up wealth in an asset, and then borrow against it when you need liquidity. But there's nothing special about *life insurance* for this. I could just as easily 'do IBC' using my house and home equity loans from a regular bank."**

ANSWER: We love this question because it allows us to demonstrate why Nelson Nash picked dividend-paying Whole Life insurance as the best vehicle with which to implement his idea of "becoming your own banker." Yes, in principle you could "do IBC" using home equity loans on your house, but let's consider what this would look like in practice.

Suppose your daughter is getting married and you need access to $20,000. You have plenty of equity in your house, so you approach your friendly commercial banker and ask for a home equity loan (HEL) of $20,000. The banker is going to ask you a battery of questions, such as: What's the loan for? What's your income? What repayment schedule are you committing to? And of course, the banker will look up your credit score. It will take some time to go through this process, even if it's successful. Finally, assuming you get the HEL, you are then committed to repaying it according to the schedule initially agreed upon. If something comes up—perhaps you get laid off or have a medical problem—and you fall behind in your payments, then (depending on the specifics) the bank might have the legal right to file a lawsuit, garnish your wages, seize other assets, or even kick you out of your house in order to foreclose on the property and pay off the note.

In complete contrast, suppose you have been practicing IBC the way Nelson Nash envisions it. Your daughter is getting married, so you call up the life insurance company and request a $20,000 policy loan. The employee of the company will not ask you what the money is for, will not ask about your income, will not ask you about a repayment plan, and will not look up your credit score. They will have the check in the mail to you probably in the next business day (or will directly deposit the funds into your checking account). Once you get the money, you can pay it back on whatever schedule you choose. If you have a tight month, no problem; you don't need to send *any* money to the life insurance company on this policy loan, if you don't want to. None of your other assets has anything to do with the policy loan; the life insurance company will not come after you to get paid back. (Remember our discussion back in Chapter 1: This contrast is why we recommended that business owners in particular set up their "alternate bank.")

How can this be possible? Do the commercial banks employ grumpy misanthropes, while the life insurance companies employ cheery idealists?

Of course not. The reason the two experiences are completely different, is that the *nature of the collateral* on the loans is different. If you take out a home equity loan, it is ultimately the market value of your house that is the lender's security, in case you don't pay back the loan. But this is still risky, from the commercial bank's perspective. For one thing, the real estate market could collapse, turning the HEL "upside down." But even if the HEL is well collateralized—meaning that the market value of your house is much higher than the balance on the HEL—it's still a cumbersome process to foreclose on a property to get the funds. In other words, houses aren't very liquid. Just because your house might be "worth $300,000" doesn't mean the commercial bank can easily turn it into $300,000 in cash, in order to pay itself back the HEL that you defaulted on. This is why the commercial bank will take steps to protect itself, before granting a home equity loan in the first place. The bank doesn't *want* to find itself in a position of having to collect on a homeowner who's behind in payments.

In contrast, recall from Chapter 3 how policy loans work: The life insurance company is granting you a loan "on the side," with the cash surrender value of your policy serving as the collateral on the loan. From the life insurance company's viewpoint, the policy loans it grants to policyholders are literally *the safest possible investment it can make.* Since the insurance company itself is guaranteeing the cash value of the policy, it provides the collateral for its own loan.

This is why the life insurance company can afford to be so "generous" and flexible in the terms of the policy loan. The company knows it will eventually be paid back—it's just not sure *when.* At some point, either the insured person will die, or the owner of the policy will decide to surrender it. At that moment, the life insurance company will pay off the outstanding policy loan balance, giving the net check as a death benefit or cash value (if the triggering event is death versus surrender of the policy). Rather than have to kick a family out of a house and foreclose on the property—as is the case with commercial banks and home equity loans—when it comes to a policy loan, the life insurance company at worst has to perform a subtraction problem before sending a check out the door.

So yes, it is true that IBC is about banking, and not about life insurance per se. In principle, you could "do IBC" with other types of assets. However, in practice the features of a dividend-paying Whole Life insurance policy make it the ideal platform for implementing IBC.

➔**QUESTION #6: "If the economy crashes, won't the life insurance companies go down too?"**

ANSWER: Of course, for a truly catastrophic economic calamity, the life insurance sector could be pulled down along with the stock market and commercial banking sector. There is no such thing as absolute security this side of the grave.

Having said that, there are *degrees* of economic calamity. Certain industries and asset classes are more vulnerable than others. For example, during the Great Depression, thousands of commercial banks failed, while the life insurance companies proved much more resilient—indeed, during the early 1930s many Americans tapped into their cash values in their life insurance policies when the regular banks were locked up. (We provide more statistics and some of the U.S. experience with life insurance in Chapter 6.)

For those readers who are (justifiably) worried about an economic crash, it is instructive to review the findings of John Exter (1910-2006), an American economist who had experience working for both the Federal Reserve and the private sector in banking. He is famous for creating "Exter's Pyramid," which summarized his research into the history of financial panics:

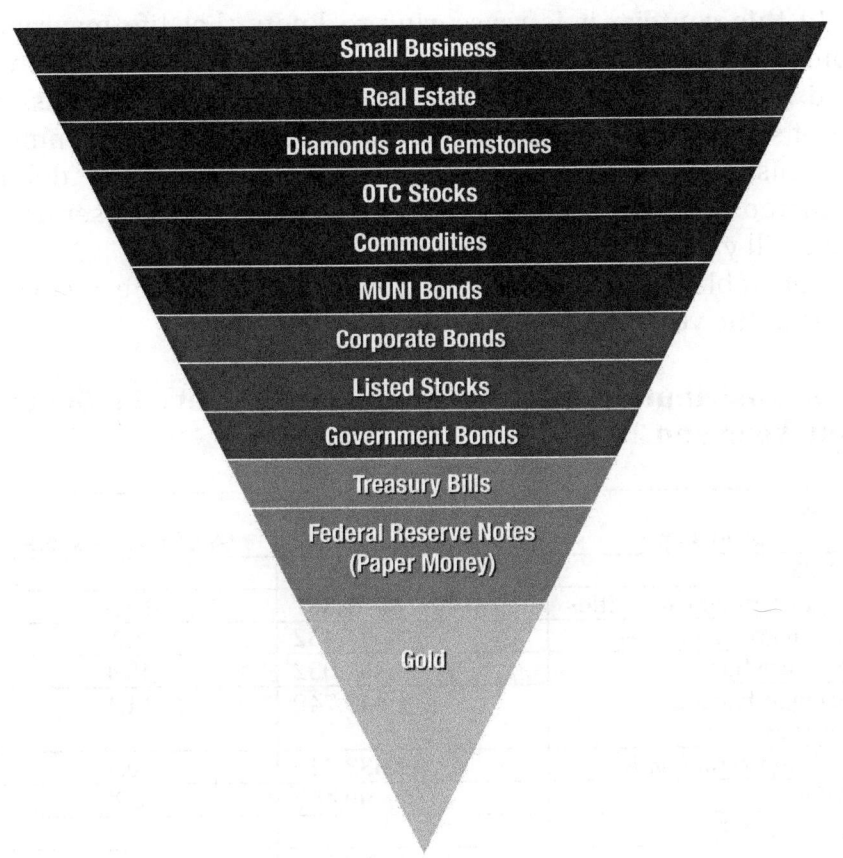

During a typical financial panic, investors dump assets at the top of the pyramid and rush to assets located toward the base of the pyramid. In general, in times of crisis investors flock to *liquidity*. They want assets that can be quickly converted into money, and that is why paper currency itself is located near the base of the pyramid. However, notice that gold is the most desirable asset to hold during a crisis; this is because the currency itself could collapse during a bout of hyperinflation. Historically, gold (and silver) were the market-produced money, and gold still fills that function by providing a safe haven for investors during times of uncertainty.

In this context, it is reassuring to know that life insurance companies invest primarily in the middle to lower segment of Exter's pyramid. Specifically, a large fraction of a typical life insurer's assets consist of safe (investment grade) corporate bonds and government bonds. This allows the insurance company to match its dollar-denominated liabilities with corresponding assets, in a conservative way that still yields a positive (if modest) return.

The table below provides a snapshot of U.S. life insurers' assets, as of the year 2015.[v]

Table 2. Distribution of U.S. Life Insurer Assets in General Account, Year-end 2015

Asset Type	Market Value (millions $)	% of Total Assets
BONDS		
U.S. government securities	$349,507	8.7%
Foreign gov. securities	77,432	1.9
Corporate bonds	1,957,032	48.4
Mortgage-backed securities	449,748	11.1
Total long-term bonds	2,833,719	70.1
STOCKS	90,452	2.2
MORTGAGES		
Farm	17,947	0.4
Residential	13,632	0.3
Commercial	383,275	9.5
Total mortgages	414,854	10.3
POLICY LOANS	129,688	3.2
Short-term investments	60,043	1.5
Cash and equivalents	46,285	1.1
TOTAL	$4,039,968	100%

SOURCE: ACLI, 2016 Fact Book, Table 2.1 (p. 11)

As the data in Table 2 reveal, the life insurance industry (as of 2015) was in a fairly defensible position, vis-à-vis Exter's Pyramid. Fully 48.4 percent of the general account assets consisted of corporate bonds, an additional 8.7 percent were U.S. government bonds, 3.2 percent were policy loans (which remember are literally the safest investment possible for a life insurance company), and another 2.6 percent were short-term assets including cash. We can summarize by saying some 63 percent of the general account[vi] assets (for 2015 data, the latest we have as of this writing) would be classified as very liquid, possessing moderate to low risk in the event of another financial crisis.

To be sure, a major crisis could knock out even Fortune 500 companies, causing them to default on their bonds, and if tax receipts collapse while requests for food stamps and other assistance skyrocket, even Uncle Sam might default. Even so, in terms of holding a collection of assets that will likely yield a modest return with as little risk as possible, the life insurers' general account is pretty balanced.

Finally, remember that IBC is not an "investment in life insurance." If you are worried about an economic crash and want to bulk up your holdings of gold, canned food, ammunition, foreign stocks, etc., then you are free to do so.

→ **QUESTION #7:** "If the commercial banking system is vulnerable—as you've explained—then why would it be safe to keep my cash in an IBC policy? Doesn't the life insurance company keep my cash in commercial banks? How can I get a policy loan if the banks are all closed?"

ANSWER: As we explained in the previous answers, you can loosely think of the "cash surrender value" as a pile of financial assets that the life insurance company maintains on behalf of the policyholder. As the cash surrender value grows over time, the market value of the assets "backing up" the policy must rise as well. (The arrangement is more complicated than a simple mutual fund, because of the possibility of death and the big payout, higher than the cash surrender value. But it's still true that the life insurance company oversees a growing pile of assets for a policy as it ages.)

Now in order to pass along a decent (implicit) rate of return on the policy, the life insurance company doesn't literally keep your "cash values" in a checking account with a commercial bank. Rather, the assets "backing up" your policy consist of financial assets—primarily conservative bonds—as outlined in our answer above to Question #6. At any moment in time, only a small fraction of a typical life insurance company's total assets is literally in the form of money on deposit in a commercial bank. Even the "cash and cash equivalents" listed on balance sheets (such as in our table above) includes holdings of Money Market Mutual Funds.

Consequently, if a panic hit the banking system and depositors couldn't access their checking account balances, this wouldn't trap very much of the typical life insurance company's wealth. The "cash surrender value" available to you at any given time shows how much cash the company would give you—either as a policy loan or as the actual surrender value if you closed the policy—but that money would be diverted from incoming premium payments, or by selling off assets. (To repeat, the life insurance company isn't literally holding cash in a commercial bank on your behalf, in order to advance you policy loans.)

Because of this structure, the strategy outlined in Chapter 1 is perfectly reasonable: business owners who wish to avoid vulnerability to a commercial banking crisis can sweep their excess balances into properly designed Whole Life insurance policies. This would not simply transfer the risk of a bank closure from the individual to the life insurance company.

Finally, let us acknowledge that *yes* you need a commercial bank in order to be able to use a policy loan from the life insurance company. To give you the loan, the company will either need to directly deposit it into your checking account, or will mail you a paper check, which you must of course deposit into a checking account.

Yet even so, the individual worried about a commercial banking crisis is still much more secure by practicing IBC. If the individual keeps a large checking account balance with a conventional bank, then *if that particular bank goes down*, the individual could be in trouble (depending on the state of the FDIC fund and the attitude of regulators towards "bail-ins"). In contrast, if the individual has most of his "cash" held in the form of cash surrender value in a large Whole Life policy, then to access his money via a policy loan he only needs *at least one bank in the entire community* to be functioning, in order to process his check. In a serious crisis where literally every commercial bank shuts down, the distinction is a moot point, but for lesser crises where only *some* of the banks remain closed, the strategy laid out in Chapter 1 gives a definite advantage in maintaining access to funds.

→ **QUESTION #8:** "If I'm worried about price inflation, then isn't life insurance a bad place to keep my money? I want to avoid dollar-denominated assets if I think the dollar might tank."

ANSWER: As we continue to stress throughout this book, Nelson Nash is *not* advising people to "invest in life insurance." Rather, he is counseling them on "becoming your own banker" through the skillful use of properly-designed Whole Life insurance policies. (As Nelson likes to ask, "If you have a checking account with a regular bank, does that mean you invested in checking?")

If you are worried about the U.S. dollar sinking against other currencies (or against real goods and services more generally), and you want to invest in traditional "inflation hedges" such as the precious metals, real estate, etc., then you are free to do so. Indeed, if you practice IBC rather than following the conventional wisdom, then you will have much more freedom in pursuing your inflation strategies. This is because it is very simple to take out a policy loan in order to (say) buy a bunch of gold coins. In contrast, if you have stored the bulk of your "retirement savings" in a 401(k) or other tax-qualified vehicle, then you may suffer stiff penalties if you want to withdraw some of that money in order to protect yourself from an outbreak of inflation.

It's also worth repeating that buying a life insurance policy is *not* the same thing as "investing in bonds." After all, life insurance and bonds are different types of financial assets, with different characteristics. When you sign a life insurance contract, it's true that the *benefits* to you are denominated in future dollars—either in the form of an eventual death benefit payment, or in the form of steadily rising cash surrender values over time. However, the *costs* to you are also denominated in future dollars—namely, you are on the hook for making a fixed premium payment for many years. It's certainly true that a sudden collapse of the U.S. dollar, and subsequent jump in price inflation rates, could make the projected cash values of your life insurance policy less attractive. On the flip side, though, it will be easier for you to make the contractually required premium payments, in an environment where the dollar is not worth as much. (Refer again to the discussion near the end of Chapter 4, regarding Nelson Nash's actual life insurance policy and how it performed amidst a falling dollar.)

➔ **QUESTION #9: "What if Congress changes the tax rules governing life insurance?"**

ANSWER: Nobody can control what Congress may do in the future. However, we have three main responses to this question.

First, IBC is not a tax gimmick. Whole Life insurance existed before the modern federal income tax (which was introduced via the 16th Amendment in 1913). Although it is certainly true that properly-designed Whole Life insurance policies enjoy certain tax advantages, those are just icing on the cake; IBC "works" on its own merits, not because of the tax code.

Second, the beneficial tax treatment of Whole Life policies is *not* due to some arbitrary loopholes that were granted on behalf of clever lobbyists. Rather, the tax treatment of life insurance makes sense, from an accounting and economic perspective. Most obvious, the death benefit payment to a beneficiary is income-tax free, because this is simply making the person whole after a loss. For an analogy, if you are in a car accident and have a $10,000 repair, then the $10,000 check that your car insurance company sends you is *not* taxable income. You haven't earned an extra $10,000 that year; instead, you've suffered a $10,000 loss for which you were made whole. It would be a fiction if the government classified such payments as income for tax purposes.

Another beneficial aspect of IBC is that—if you conduct your affairs properly—then policy loans are not treated as taxable income. This isn't a "loophole," though, because it makes perfect sense. When you take out a policy loan, that is not net income in an accounting sense; you gain an asset (the check from the insurance company) but you also suffer from an equal liability (your debt to the insurance company). If you take out a $20,000 loan, that is *not* the same thing as earning a $20,000 bonus from your employer, and it would be crazy for the IRS to treat them the same. (Of course, reason and logic never stopped the Congress from passing silly tax legislation in the past. But our point is that there is a rationale behind the current tax treatment of life insurance.)

Third, even if Congress changes the rules to make the tax treatment of Whole Life policies less advantageous, the new rules might only apply to *new* policies issued after the change. When Congress changed the tax treatment of life insurance in the late 1980s, they grandfathered in the already-existing policies. (We discuss this more in Chapter 6.) As of this writing, there is debate over a major tax overhaul that may change the deductibility of interest on home mortgages, but the debate is confined to *newly issued* mortgages. People who bought houses and took out mortgages under the old rule, will not have the rug pulled out from under them (though the value of their house will reflect new rules if they try to sell).

➔**QUESTION #10:** "Why do you insist on implementing IBC with a Whole Life policy? Couldn't you 'become your own banker' with a Universal Life or other permanent life insurance policy?"

ANSWER: The point of IBC is to "become your own banker," and as we explained in Chapter 1, the goal is to set up an alternate "bank" that is a superior warehouse for your wealth (the title of Nelson Nash's follow-up book). Consequently, those permanent life insurance products that are designed to have exposure to the stock market—such as an Equity Indexed Universal Life policy—don't really make sense for people who are trying to shield themselves from the volatility of the equity markets.

Now it's true that a plain vanilla Universal Life (UL) policy is, at a high level, comparable in many respects to a Whole Life policy. However, there *are* differences, and these explain why Nelson Nash insists that IBC is implemented with a Whole Life policy, *not* a UL (let alone a Variable UL or other such hybrids).

It is beyond the scope of this book to enter into a detailed comparison of the various life insurance products. Suffice it to say that with a Universal Life policy, the uncertainty—which can be good or bad—is left on the policyholder, whereas with a Whole Life policy, the policyholder is offered more guarantees, with the company bearing the uncertainty (good or bad).

With a Whole Life policy, the customer knows that so long as he or she makes the specified contractual premium payments, the policy will grow *at least* as much as depicted in the "guaranteed" illustration. In contrast, there are plenty of real-world "horror stories" with Universal Life policies, where the customer had the flexibility of lowering his premium contribution during a high interest rate period, but didn't pay attention and eventually got a letter informing him that his policy had cannibalized itself and was on the verge of collapse. To repeat, this type of scenario doesn't occur with a Whole Life policy, which has a fixed premium schedule and minimum levels of a steadily rising, guaranteed cash value. If the life insurance portfolio performs better than expected, then the policyholder can "participate" in the good times through dividend payments, but the basic structure of a Whole Life contract is very *boring*—which is exactly what you want when setting up an alternate "bank."

The Economics of IBC

➔ **QUESTION #11: "This makes a lot of sense...for people who are younger/older than me."**

ANSWER: There's nothing in Nelson Nash's arguments that has to do with age. If it makes sense for a 28-year-old to become his own banker, then it also makes sense for a 58-year-old.

Naturally, the *way* you become your own banker will be different, depending on your specific circumstances. A young person (especially if a new parent) may not have very much disposable income to set aside for building up an IBC policy. Even so, on the bright side a young person has decades in which the magic of compounding can go to work. We, the authors of this book, have met countless middle-aged people who lament to us, "Why didn't I hear about IBC twenty years ago?!"

On the other hand, people who are in their 60s or older will have to pay high premiums for the "pure cost of insurance,"[vii] and they may not have labor income anymore. Even so, if they have other assets and wish to fund a Whole Life policy, there are ways of doing so. However, you should be aware that there are specific rules that must be followed to avoid disadvantageous tax treatment of the policy, and financial professionals must be very careful not to cross any lines when rendering guidance on such matters. This is why it is so important to work with qualified individuals when considering IBC.

In this book and our other public outreach efforts, we are speaking in broad generalities. If you want to pursue Nelson Nash's ideas and learn how to apply them in your own life, you should contact one of the Authorized IBC Practitioners who have been through our training program. They are listed at: www.InfiniteBanking.org/Finder.

[i] For a comprehensive critique, see the article "Why Dave Ramsey Is Wrong About Whole Life," in the September 2012 issue of the *Lara-Murphy Report*, available at: https://lara-murphy.com/wp-content/uploads/lmr_september2012.pdf.

[ii] Indeed, Ramsey claims that this is fine because the individual will "self-insure" at that point—which is a fancy way of saying the individual won't have life insurance!

[iii] In Chapter 7, we give some more specifics about the design of a modern IBC policy, in which a base premium is supplemented with contributions to a "paid up additions" rider.

[iv] In practice, there are state-based regulations governing the minimum cash surrender values at each point in the policy, specified contractually. But in the text above we are just trying to get the reader to understand the economic logic underlying these numbers.

[v] The table and following commentary are adapted from the analysis in Robert Murphy's article in the August 2017 *Lara-Murphy Report*.

[vi] The *general account* of a life insurance company holds the assets needed to provide death benefit payments and other insurance-related expenses, whereas the *separate account* (the data on which are not shown in the table) holds the assets related to special products that serve as investment pass-through vehicles, such as variable annuities or Variable Universal Life (VUL) insurance policies. For people practicing IBC who are worried about the health of the life insurance sector, the strength of the general account assets is all that matters.

[vii] Even though it's true that a given premium payment won't support as high a death benefit—other things equal—for a 60-year-old new applicant as compared to a 30-year-old new applicant, keep in mind that it's the *cash value* available that determines usefulness for IBC purposes.

Chapter 6
Lessons From History

We've given you, the reader, a lot of *theory* so far in this book, but let's turn now to some *history*. Specifically, we'll describe some of the major changes in our financial system that help explain why the business owner in Chapter 1 found himself in such a vice. You'll also see that the knock against Whole Life insurance is a relatively recent phenomenon.

For a fuller treatment of these issues, consult Lara and Murphy's book, *How Privatized Banking **Really** Works*. But in this chapter we will give you the basics to understand the historical context of our message to business owners and households.

The Gold Standard and Whole Life

Historically, the average household used life insurance as a savings vehicle. The great Austrian School economist Ludwig von Mises, in his 1949 treatise *Human Action*, writes matter-of-factly: "*For those not personally engaged in business and not familiar with the conditions of the stock market, the main vehicle of saving is the accumulation of savings deposits, the purchase of bonds and life insurance*" (Mises p. 547).

Later in the book Mises goes on to argue:

> [Under capitalism, even] for those with moderate incomes the opportunity is offered, by saving and insurance policies, to provide for accidents, sickness, old age, the education of their children, and the support of widows and orphans. It is highly probable that the funds

of the charitable institutions would be sufficient in the capitalist countries if interventionism were not to sabotage the essential institutions of the market economy. **Credit expansion and inflationary increase of the quantity of money frustrate the "common man's" attempts to save** *and to accumulate reserves for less propitious days.* (Mises 1949, p. 834, bold added.)

Even at that early point, Mises had already put his finger on a disturbing trend: the increase in government intervention in the economy—particularly when it came to money and banking—undermined the ability of the private sector to provide for the financial security of the general public. In a vicious cycle, political interference would hamper the market's ability to care for the elderly, widows, the poor, etc., and then the politicians would point to this "market failure" as proof of the need for their interference!

Mises developed an explanation of how government intervention in the banking system causes the boom-bust cycle that plagues market economies. His disciple Friedrich Hayek in 1974 would win the Nobel Prize in economics for elaborating on Mises' work. However, though Mises' explanation is crucial for understanding our modern economy, the topic can be technical and lies outside the scope of our present discussion. (Consult www.Lara-Murphy.com for a quick explanation and links for more comprehensive study.) But we *will* explain the major events concerning the gold standard, since it affected the fortunes of Whole Life insurance so significantly.

Before World War I, all major countries were on the classical gold standard. This meant that they tied their national currencies (the British pound, the French franc, the German mark, the U.S. dollar, etc.) to a fixed weight of gold. *Anybody* could present the national currency and redeem it for the stipulated amount of gold.

These fixed rates vis-à-vis gold then implied an "anchor" for the exchange rates between the respective currencies. For example, under the classical gold standard, the British government promised to redeem 4.25 British pounds for an ounce of gold. At the same time, the U.S. government redeemed dollars at $20.67 per ounce of gold.

This implied an exchange rate of $4.86 per British pound. And indeed, if the actual conditions on the forex market moved the USD/British pound exchange rate away from this anchor point, then eventually speculators would enter the scene, trading the currencies and moving gold from one country to the other, to push the exchange rate toward the anchor point and keep the "inflating" country more honest.[i]

The classical gold standard was destroyed during World War I, when most of the belligerents abandoned the redemption of their currencies for gold. However, in the United States the first major blow occurred when Franklin D. Roosevelt assumed office in early 1933. Elected during the depths of the Great Depression, FDR engaged in "emergency" action, which included a nationwide "bank holiday"[ii] and required Americans to turn in their gold, under pain of a huge fine and/or prison sentence! By the following year, the Roosevelt Administration would "revalue" gold at the stable price of $35 per ounce, but even here only foreign governments and central banks could turn in their dollars for gold; regular citizens could no longer do so.

After World War II, the major nations participated in the so-called Bretton Woods framework, in which the U.S. dollar was the major reserve underpinning all other currencies. However, even here there was still an ultimate check on the Federal Reserve's ability to print dollars, because these foreign institutions had the right to redeem $35 for an ounce of gold. This reassured them that the Americans couldn't be too reckless in their creation of dollars, and so it seemed reasonable to switch to a global financial system based on a dollar reserve, rather than the gold reserves that had prevailed before the first Great War.

Eventually, even this last vestige of the classical gold standard was swept away. Fueled by the deficit financing of the Vietnam War and the "Great Society" welfare programs of the 1960s, the U.S. government's financial position became untenable. Faced with the choice of cutting spending or abandoning the dollar's tie to gold, Richard Nixon made the fateful decision in August 1971 to "close the gold window." From this point forward, no one—not even central bankers from other major governments—could redeem U.S. dollars for gold. At this point, the U.S. and hence the whole world, was on a system of "fiat money," meaning paper currencies backed up by nothing.

What was the result of Nixon's decision to take the dollar off of gold? The surge in price inflation later in the 1970s. It is not surprising that when the U.S. government removed the shackles from the printing press, all of a sudden it seemed America had an inflation problem.

This radical transformation in American monetary policy had a profound effect on the financial behavior of ordinary households. The dollar-denominated guarantees of Whole Life insurance were seen as less reliable once consumer prices began increasing at high and unpredictable rates. Especially with the innovation of mutual funds, the conventional wisdom eventually argued that the "smart move" was putting one's savings into Wall Street. The move to Wall Street was also encouraged by the 1974 ERISA legislation and subsequent rise of "tax-qualified" retirement plans. (Obviously, we are not *endorsing* this change in mindset concerning Whole Life versus the stock market, as our earlier chapters indicate.) And for those who wanted liquidity, short-term bank CDs seemed a better bet amidst high and volatile price inflation, since investors could jump in and out of the short-term market depending on interest rates. In contrast, people holding mature Whole Life policies would be reaping returns based on portfolios of "old" bonds, issued at a time when price inflation had not been so volatile.

The following table distills our historical narrative. The table first shows the total increase (measured in historical, non-inflation-adjusted dollars) in financial assets among U.S. individuals during various years; this reflects the total amount of saving (broadly defined) in financial assets for those years. Then the table shows the percentage of that total saving accruing in different financial instruments.

Table 3. Increase in Market Value of Individuals' Financial Assets, Total and By Components, 1950 – 1985

Year	Total Increase in Financial Assets (historical billions $)	Portion of Total Annual Increase Due to...							
		Life Insurance Reserves	Currency and Demand Deposits	Time and Savings Deposits	US Federal Gov't Bonds	Corp. and Foreign Bonds	Private Pension (insured and uninsured)	Gov't Insurance and Pension Reserves	Mutual Fund Shares
1950	$13.7	19%	16%	18%	-1%	-6%	18%	13%	n/a
1955	$27.9	11%	3%	32%	9%	4%	13%	6%	n/a
1960	$27.7	11%	-7%	45%	-2%	1%	19%	12%	n/a
1965	$56.0	8%	13%	47%	4%	1%	14%	9%	n/a
1970	$80.5	6%	11%	54%	-6%	13%	13%	11%	2%
1975	$179.3	4%	3%	43%	9%	5%	27%	8%	0%
1980	$320.3	3%	3%	39%	6%	-4%	23%	11%	0%
1985	$543.8	2%	7%	23%	15%	0%	19%	13%	13%

SOURCES:[iii] *Statistical Abstract of the United States* (No. 709, Flow of Funds Accounts) and *Historical Statistics, Colonial Times to 1970* (Series F 566-594, Individuals' Saving)

As the table indicates, in 1950 the portion of individual saving in financial assets attributable to life insurance was 19%, higher than any of the other components listed. But by 1985, the share of financial saving in the form of life insurance had dwindled to 2%. Time and savings deposits, and later on mutual funds, eventually seemed much more attractive to individual households amidst the uncertainty of the postwar era.

The FTC Report

So far we have explained why life insurance in general fell out of favor with the American public, but *Whole Life* insurance in particular suffered a major blow in 1979, when a scathing Federal Trade Commission (FTC) report castigated Whole Life as a poor savings instrument that provided paltry returns and lack of information for the consumer. Activists such as Ralph Nader jumped into the fray, declaring that, "Policies are not sold on the basis of consumer need, but on the basis of industry greed."[iv]

At the time, actuaries and other experts complained that the FTC report was based on incorrect or misleading calculations, but the damage had been done: In the life insurance sector, the share of Whole Life went from 85% in 1979 to 50% by 1986, with its fall being almost perfectly counterbalanced by the rise of "Universal Life" (UL).[v] This was a newer product that promised the same benefits of Whole Life, but with more flexibility and transparency. In the high interest rate environment of the early 1980s, new UL policies seemed superior to previously issued Whole Life policies, but this proved illusory for many consumers once interest rates fell.

The 1986 Tax Reform Act

The next episode in our historical survey concerns the 1986 Tax Reform Act. This was a major overhaul of the U.S. tax code that continued the "supply-side" revolution that began when Ronald Reagan had first been elected in 1980. When all was said and done, the U.S. personal income tax code went from having *seventeen* brackets with a top marginal rate of *70 percent* in 1980, down to a tax code with only *two* brackets and a top marginal rate of *28 percent* in 1988.[vi]

Part of the logic of the tax cut / reform program of the 1980s was to reduce the *rate* of taxation while broadening the *base*. In this way—so the argument went—individuals and businesses would make economic decisions on the basis of market prices, rather than the tax code. Rather than "picking winners and losers," the tax code would take a uniform (and as small as possible) cut off the top of *all* activities, letting the private sector arrange its affairs within that neutral framework.

It is not our place to praise or condemn the merits of this philosophy. What the sweeping 1986 Tax Reform Act did—among other things—was to remove "real estate tax shelters" that had been very attractive to investors, especially following the wild bouts of price inflation of the 1970s and then the severe recession of the early 1980s. (In accordance with Mises' explanation of the business cycle, these two events were related.) By "closing loopholes" in the 1986 reform, all of a sudden, investors were left holding real estate investments that were not nearly as valuable—in after-tax terms—as they had been before. Consequently, the real estate market crashed. And on October 19, 1987, investors suffered "Black Monday," when the Dow Jones fell more than a staggering 22%—the worst single-day drop (in percentage terms) in stock market history.

The Wealthy Return to Whole Life

In this environment, the nation's elite were nonplussed. They had just been burned by real estate and equities, and even commodities (such as gold and oil) had crashed from their inflation-driven peaks earlier in the decade. The sweeping tax reform, though welcome in terms of rate reductions, had eliminated the advantages of some of their favorite financial moves. Where should they put their money now? The wealthy elite turned to their experts on retainer for guidance.

In this new world, believe it or not, the high-priced tax attorneys came back to their clients and advised them: "Write one big check and put it into a single-premium Whole Life insurance policy."

Naturally, the nation's wealthy were stunned. Didn't everybody know that Whole Life was a terrible place to put your money? And yet, the advisors walked through the same basic considerations that we ourselves have covered in Chapter 2 of this book. To paraphrase Winston Churchill: Sure, Whole Life is the worst possible investment—except for all the others.

And so it was that many of the richest Americans began writing checks for "paid up" Whole Life insurance policies. They were a conservative, reputable vehicle that offered modest but consistent (and guaranteed) returns, with favorable tax treatment, and yet also provided liquidity in the form of policy loans. After being seduced by the stock market and real estate, many wealthy Americans rediscovered what their grandparents knew.

"MEC" Status and the 7-Pay Test

Indeed, such was the stampede for permanent life insurance policies that Congress held hearings on the matter. They became concerned that too many wealthy Americans were using life insurance as a way to minimize their tax bills, rather than serving to provide for widows and orphans.

To cut a long story short, the 1988 Technical and Miscellaneous Revenue Act (TAMRA) denied many (though not all) of the tax advantages to those life insurance policies deemed a "Modified Endowment Contract" (MEC). To be clear, a policy that is deemed a MEC is still classified as life insurance, but it is treated tax-wise more as an investment vehicle and loses many of the benefits available to a life insurance policy that avoids the MEC classification.

In the industry, the so-called "7-pay test" is used to ensure that a life insurance policy is not classified as a MEC. This criterion is applied when a new policy is opened, or any time an existing policy undergoes a "material change." Loosely speaking, the 7-pay test means that for seven years, the *cumulative* amount of premium paid into a life insurance policy at any point cannot exceed the cumulative amount that would have been paid (by that point) in a life insurance policy with the same death benefit, and that was also designed to be fully paid-up after seven years. This rule is very strict, in the sense that once a policy is declared a MEC, it cannot be undone. In particular, if too much money is paid in premiums early on during the 7-year period, the owner of the policy can't "balance it out" by smaller premium payments afterward. Once a MEC, always a MEC.

Intuitively, the purpose of the government's refinements of the tax code was to limit the ability of wealthy individuals to move large amounts of money into life insurance policies in one fell swoop. In order to take full advantage of the tax treatment afforded to traditional life insurance, policyholders must pay premiums into their policies over a period of at least seven years.

The following slide summarizes some of the most salient elements of our historical narrative:

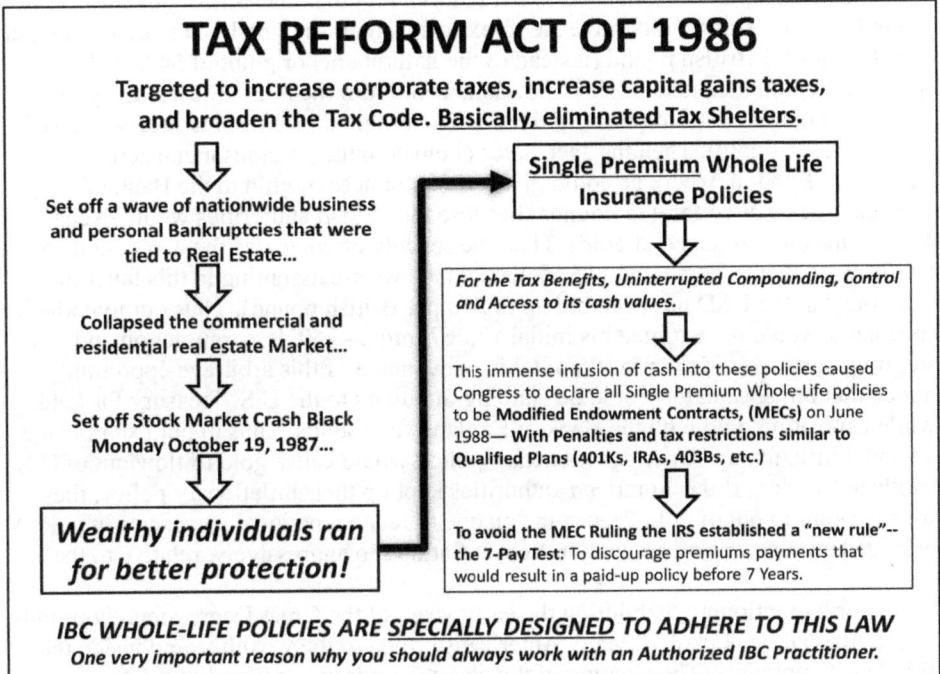

Conclusion

There are two take-away messages from our historical summary. First, there is nothing foolish about using Whole Life policies as part of one's financial planning. This was standard for American households through the 1950s, and after in the late 1980s Congress had to take action to *discourage* rich people from putting so much of their money into permanent life insurance! (How does Dave Ramsey explain *that*?)

Second, there are many subtleties involved with the proper design of a Whole Life policy that is intended to serve "banking" purposes. This is why any reader interested in discussing these matters further should consult one of our Authorized IBC Practitioners.

---

[i] A numerical example will illustrate the mechanism by which the classical gold standard kept national governments (relatively) "honest." Suppose the American government had printed dollars far more aggressively than the British government had printed pounds. This would move the forex rate so that, say, the USD traded at the rate of $10 against 1 British pound (instead of the natural anchor point of $4.86). A speculator could then take $2,067 U.S. dollars and turn them into the Treasury to obtain 100 ounces of gold (because the U.S. government promised to redeem $20.67 for an ounce of gold). Then the speculator could ship the precious metal across the Atlantic to London, where he could give the 100 ounces of gold to the Bank of England in exchange for 425 pounds (because the British authorities would exchange 4.25 pounds for an ounce of gold). Then the speculator could use the 425 pounds on the forex market to buy 4,250 U.S. dollars (since we are assuming in this fanciful example that the USD has been bid up to $10 per British pound). Thus our hypothetical speculator would have turned his initial $2,067 into $4,250, less transaction and shipping costs. But in the process of taking advantage of this arbitrage opportunity, notice that our speculator would be handing in dollars to the U.S. Treasury for gold, while depositing gold with the Bank of England for pounds. Thus in our example the assumed inflationary American monetary policy would cause gold to flow out of U.S. vaults to London. If the American authorities kept up their inflationary policy, they would soon run out of gold. Hence the pledge to redeem national currencies in gold provided a check on any one nation from inflating too aggressively, relative to the others.

[ii] It's worth mentioning that during the early years of the Great Depression, thousands of commercial banks failed. Many Americans turned to the wealth stored inside their Whole Life policies. (The opening of the classic movie *It's a Wonderful Life* showcases both elements of this history.)

[iii] Regarding Table 3, the numbers for the total dollar amount of "individual" financial asset increase are not exactly comparable between 1950-1965 and 1970-1985, because the definition of "individual" financial entities slightly changed once we switch to 1970 going forward. However, the numbers are close, and the percentages of the components (which is the real message of the table for our narrative) across time are quite comparable.

[iv] Nader quote available at: http://en.wikiquote.org/wiki/Talk:Ralph_Nader.

[v] See Kenneth Black and Harold D. Skipper, *Life Insurance* (12th Edition), p. 83.

[vi] The history of the U.S. personal income tax brackets and rates is available at: https://files.taxfoundation.org/legacy/docs/fed_individual_rate_history_nominal.pdf.

Chapter 7
Putting IBC Into Action

So far in this book, we've outlined the financial problem gripping the typical business owner and household. We've explained that IBC is the solution, and we taught you the basics of dividend-paying Whole Life insurance, which is the platform you use to implement IBC. We also dealt with common objections and concerns, and we then provided some historical background for our discussion.

With all of that groundwork, we are now in a position to show you *one example* of putting IBC into action. Remember, Nelson Nash named it the *Infinite* Banking Concept, to stress that you are only limited by your imagination. The point of IBC isn't to "put your money in life insurance," instead it's to hold your liquid funds in this very convenient vehicle, before you *deploy it* to achieve your specific goals.

We started this book by looking at things from the perspective of a business owner. It is only fitting, therefore, that we end the book the same way. However, we hope that the following analysis sheds light on the power of IBC, not just for the successful business owner, but for any household. (Let us repeat yet again that the interested reader should be sure to consult Nash's original book, *Becoming Your Own Banker*, for further examples of "IBC in action.")

"IBC sounds great, if I weren't so strapped right now..."

In our experience, as we explained way back in Chapter 1, business owners typically see the benefits of IBC right away. However, even though they appreciate the advantages of an "alternate bank" and cashflow management system, oftentimes the business owner will say to us, *"I agree that this makes a lot of sense, and if I had a bunch of extra money each month that I could consistently earmark for this, sure I'd start aggressively funding a policy like you* are talking about. But my cashflow comes and goes, and if I were to set up a policy small enough that I could be sure I'd always have enough for the premium, then it would take forever to get off the ground and become large enough to accommodate the banking needs of my business."

It was in response to *this* typical reaction that we developed the strategy in this chapter. Again we want to stress, this is just *one example* of how a business owner might use IBC. It is not at all necessary that "if you do IBC, it should look like this." We are merely trying to show that the business owner who pushes back in the above fashion, hasn't yet fully realized the power and flexibility of IBC.

Using a Recurring Expense to Build the Infrastructure of an IBC Policy

The basic maneuver we are going to use in this example is to take a large, predictable expense for the business owner. (This is part of the reason the owner feels that he has so little margin for error, because he has expenses like *these* that are always going out the door.) Then, before the business owner writes the check for this expense and kisses it goodbye, he *first* routes the amount as a payment into a Whole Life policy. If the policy is correctly designed with this strategy in mind, its cash value will increase significantly because of this payment. Then the business owner takes out a policy loan for the amount needed to pay the recurring expense. Intuitively, what happens is that the money originally earmarked for the expense ends up being used for that original purpose, but it first takes a "detour" through the Whole Life policy.

In the next section we are going to show you numbers that are based on an actual illustration developed circa 2016, when interest rates were still low compared to historical norms. Yet before we do so, we want to mention two caveats to avoid potential confusion:

First of all, *IBC is not magic*. We have not discovered a money pump or a perpetual motion machine. There isn't a tree shooting out free wealth if you adopt this strategy. We will point out some specifics along the way, but keep in mind throughout this discussion that you aren't obtaining benefits "for nothing." As we will see, there is some "drag" where the business owner has to kick in extra money in order to get the whole operation up and running. However, we think you'll agree with us that the tradeoffs are much better than our modest and cash-strapped business owner (from above) initially feared.

Our second caveat is that we are picking *taxes* as our recurring business expense, but we are *not* saying that the strategy of this chapter has anything to do with reducing your tax liability. Now it's true, if you implement IBC optimally, you will achieve your financial goals in a way that probably reduces your taxes. But that's not what we're doing in this chapter. Rather, we are simply picking an expense that is recurring, and taxes qualify on that score. We *could* have chosen items like rent or payroll as our recurring business expense, but that would have involved an extra complication of the business borrowing money from the individual (who owns the Whole Life policy[i]). Since the business owner in our example flows the business profit to himself as income on which he has to pay personal taxes, we can keep things simpler (for this introductory discussion) by picking taxes as the recurring expense.

With these important caveats out of the way, let us proceed to the actual numbers. Here is the power and flexibility of IBC, even in an environment of historically low interest rates.

An Example of IBC in Action: Diverting Tax Payments Through a Policy

Suppose we have a business owner who has been convinced of the elegance of IBC, but who can really only commit to putting, say, $20,000 per year into a properly structured Whole Life policy for "banking" purposes. Over a five- to ten-year horizon, the business owner explains that he will have significantly higher amounts of net income ($1 million+) flowing through his operation, coming in from the sale of properties and the completion of other projects. This business owner is somewhat frustrated, because if he starts an IBC policy for only $20,000 per year, then that really won't do much to reduce his dependence on commercial banks (as we discussed in Chapter 1); his business in a typical year might need to tap a "line of credit" of at least several hundred thousands of dollars. On the other hand, the business owner thinks he can't take out a policy where the premium is high enough to quickly bulk up the cash value to the ranges he desires, since—as we explained—his business income is too volatile, year to year. He can commit to earmarking $20,000 per year for a new IBC policy without problem, but beyond that, he isn't sure *when* those additional bursts of income will show up, so he doesn't want to overextend himself.

It is in this type of scenario—which is very common in our discussions with business owners, adjusting the specific numbers to their situation—that our example is applicable. Suppose upon further discussion our business owner explains that he typically has $100,000 in tax payments he must make, on the personal income that he earns as owner of the business. In this case, we can design an IBC policy that will allow the owner to accommodate payments into the policy of at least $100,000, so that the owner can then borrow $100,000 out in order to pay his tax when due.

The following table (to reiterate) is based on an actual life insurance illustration produced circa 2016, which was designed with our scenario in mind (and assumes the business owner is a 45-year-old in good health). We want to stress that *there are several "moving parts" that went into the design of this policy*, including a 30-year "term rider" (which supplements the base Whole Life policy with a term policy for the first 30 years). For an introductory book that is geared to the general public, we will not get into the weeds to explain each component of this policy's design, though we outline some specifics in our discussion below. (These real-world complications are yet more proof of the importance of talking to a financial professional who has been through our training program, before trying to implement IBC for your own business or household.)

Without further ado, here are the numbers for a policy designed with our hypothetical business owner in mind:

Table 4. Whole Life Insurance Policy Illustration for 45-year-old, circa 2016

Age	Premium	Loan Amount (during year)	Cumulative Loan Balance (includes interest)	Net Premium Outlay	Annual Dividend (rolled back into policy)	Net Cash Value (accounts for loan balance)	Net Death Benefit (accounts for loan balance)
46	$120k	$0	$0	$120,000	$900	$98,000	$2.5m
47	$120k	$93k	$98,000	$27,000	$1,900	$103k	$2.7m
48	$120k	$93k	$201,000	$27,000	$2,900	$122k	$2.9m
49	$120k	$100k	$316,000	$20,000	$3,900	$135k	$3.1m
50	$120k	$100k	$436,000	$20,000	$5,000	$147k	$3.3m
51	$120k	$100k	$563,000	$20,000	$6,200	$158k	$3.4m
52	$120k	$100k	$696,000	$20,000	$7,700	$169k	$3.6m
53	$120k	$100k	$836,000	$20,000	$9,200	$179k	$3.7m
54	$120k	$100k	$983,000	$20,000	$11,000	$188k	$3.8m
55	$120k	$100k	$1.1m	$20,000	$13,000	$196k	$4.0m
56	$20k	$0	$1.2m	$20,000	$14,200	$209k	$3.9m
57	$20k	$0	$1.3m	$20,000	$15,300	$223k	$3.9m
58	$20k	$0	$1.3m	$20,000	$16,400	$236k	$3.9m
59	$20k	$0	$1.4m	$20,000	$17,400	$248k	$3.8m
60	$20k	$0	$1.5m	$20,000	$18,500	$260k	$3.8m
...	...	...	...	...	...	...	...
75	$20k	$0	$3.0m	$20k	$44,900	$241k	$3.0m
76	$16k	$0	$3.2m	$16k	$47,000	$215k	$1.8m
77	$16k	$0	$3.3m	$16k	$49,300	$184k	$1.7m

Discussion of Table 4

The table shows the basic "infrastructure" of a (potentially) large IBC policy that is primed for our hypothetical business owner, waiting for his "fat" years when he will have large amounts of income that he wanted to flow through his "alternate bank." So to be crystal clear, the table above does *not* show the owner putting in the erratic bursts of income ("windfalls") when they occur. Instead, the table shows the policy structure that is calibrated to suit this business

Putting IBC Into Action

owner's special circumstances. Let's walk through some of the numbers to understand this example.

Start with the "Premium" column. It consists of an annual $16,000 premium for the "base" Whole Life policy that is paid up at age 100 (though we don't see this far into the policy, in the table above). This base component carries with it an initial death benefit of $1 million. In the table, you can see for ages 76 and 77 that the premium paid is only $16,000; this is the premium on the base Whole Life policy.

In addition, for the first 30 years of the policy, there is a 30-year "term rider" appended, which carries an annual premium of $4,000 and adds additional death benefit (during the years it is in force) of $1.2 million. Notice in the table that going from age 75 into age 76 makes the premium payment drop from $20,000 down to $16,000. This drop is due to the 30-year term rider expiring. It also explains why the death benefit drops from $3 million down to $1.8 million between those two years; the $1.2 million of additional death benefit coverage has expired with the 30-year term policy. (We will emphasize this point again in the text below, but let us point out that in these illustrations, the cash surrender value and death benefit figures shown in the tables are *net* of any policy loans that are outstanding in those years. In other words, the figures depict the available cash and the death benefit that will be paid out, even *after* the policy loan is paid off.)

Continuing our analysis of Table 4: The last component of the "Premium" column is the additional $100,000 that was designed to flow into the policy during its first ten years. Specifically, these payments employ a "level paid-up additions" rider, which allows the policyholder to purchase additional, fully paid-up Whole Life insurance coverage. This type of premium payment raises the cash surrender value much more quickly than a premium payment on the "base" Whole Life policy. Indeed, you can see that in the first year of the policy—where we don't take out any loans—the available cash at the end of the year is $98,000, compared to $120,000 that the man paid out-of-pocket as premium into the policy in that first year. *Notice how much of the premium payment is available for policy loans even after the first year!* If you read about Whole Life insurance on the internet, you will probably see people "explaining" that you can't start accessing your cash until several years into the policy, but such writers are unfamiliar with optimal policy design for IBC purposes.

Cross-referencing the death benefit column, we can deduce that the $100,000 premium infusion for paid-up life insurance gains some $300,000 in death benefit coverage on our hypothetical business owner in the first year. Thus, at the end of the first year, the total death benefit coverage is $1 million from the base Whole Life policy (which carries a premium of $16,000), plus $1.2 million from the 30-year term policy (which carries a premium of $4,000), plus $300,000 in death benefit coverage from that year's purchase of paid-up Whole Life insurance (which carries a premium of $100,000, and this component also catches the small contribution of the $900 dividend payment that is rolled back into the policy). Thus the *total* death benefit coverage at the end of the first year is $1.0m + $1.2m + $0.3m = $2.5 million.

In addition to these explicit premium payments, this policy is also designed such that any dividend payments (shown in the sixth column) are used to purchase additional paid-up life insurance. This is an additional factor causing the cash value and death benefit to be higher, as the policy ages.

Now consider the "Net Premium Outlay" column. This shows the *out-of-pocket* payments that the business owner must make, to build up the policy's infrastructure in the way we desire. Look at the years corresponding to Age 49 through 55. Here, the business owner puts in total premium payments of $120,000, but he takes out policy loans of $100,000 (in order to pay his tax bill). So on *net* he only kicks in $20,000 to the policy out of his cashflow, which is why the Net Premium Outlay is $20,000 for these years.

Look at the first three years to see that the business owner's net premium outlays are higher than $20,000—and in fact it is the full $120,000 in the first year of the policy. The specific numbers in the table are somewhat arbitrary, but we want to be sure the reader understands that the actual out-of-pocket infusions into the policy shown in Table 4 are greater than the basic $20,000 in the first three years.[ii]

To be clear, our business owner *could* borrow against that initial $98,000 in cash value fairly soon after his premium payment, even in the first year of the policy, and in fact that's what the business owner in our hypothetical story *would* do. But to keep things cleaner in Year 1 for the reader's comprehension, and also to make sure we illustrate how much is available for borrowing right away, we deliberately do not have the business owner borrowing against the policy in the first year, in our numbers in the table. Our decision means that the illustrated cash surrender values in Table 4, in later years, are of course higher than they would be if the business owner *had* borrowed money in the first year.

Turn your attention now to the cash column. Notice that *even in this bare-bones framework*, the business owner has a steadily rising amount of *net* cash available to borrow if he desires. In other words, the cash amounts shown in the table *already take into account* the growing loan balance.

It is also worth emphasizing that the death benefit column too is a *net* figure, taking account of the outstanding loan balance. For example, suppose the business owner dies at age 50. The life insurance company will first pay off the $436,000 outstanding policy loan balance, but there will still be $3.3 million left over to flow income-tax-free to the beneficiaries named in the policy. (In other words, the *gross* death benefit at this point in the policy was $3.7 million.)

A Place to Put "Windfalls" (Above-Normal Income)

Now that we've discussed some of the details of our table, let's remember what the original purpose was: Our business owner wants a place to put his revenues, during years when his business does particularly well. The problem (we recall) was that such "good times" were sporadic. The business owner knew they would occur over the coming decade or two, but he couldn't plan on precisely *when*.

Look again at the table, this time focusing on the "Cumulative Loan Balance" column. To people unfamiliar with IBC, these growing numbers might cause alarm. But when we understand the *purpose and context* of this particular policy design, those growing loan balances are actually a big "Welcome" mat. It shows how much cash in a given year the business owner can divert to his policy, in order to bolster both the (net) cash value and (net) death benefit.

For example, suppose at age 53 the business owner unloads a piece of property and flows $700,000 (after-tax) to himself after the sale. If he desires, he can use that money to pay down his $836,000 outstanding policy loan balance (so that it is now only $136,000). That move will make his net cash available jump from the $179,000 shown in the table up to $879,000, and his net death benefit jump from the $3.7 million shown in the table to $4.4 million.

Let us be clear to avoid confusion: In this specific example, our business owner is *not* making a premium payment of $700,000, and he is *not* "putting that money into his policy." What is *actually* happening is that he is merely paying $700,000 *to the life insurance company* to reduce the outstanding balance on the loans they've been advancing to him over the years. But since that outstanding loan balance acts as a lien against the gross Cash Surrender Value and gross Death Benefit available from the policy, in practice it's "as if" the man can boost his cash and death benefit by $700,000 through such a payment.

Putting IBC Into Action

Thus we see the versatility of IBC, so long as the underlying Whole Life policy has been correctly designed with the owner's specific circumstances in mind. Had the business owner only plowed the "Net Premium Outlay" amounts into a policy all along, by age 53 he would not have been able to accommodate his $700,000 windfall. But with our clever design shown above, our business owner can get a very sizeable policy up and running, laying down an "infrastructure" that can accommodate his "fat years" when they occur down the road.

Now That the Mind Is Opened, a Larger Policy...

As we mentioned earlier in this chapter, in the real world we wouldn't *stop* with the illustration (depicted in Table 4) that we have shown our hypothetical business owner. The primary purpose of that was to "shock" the owner into realizing the power and flexibility of IBC. Once the business owner sees the possibilities as demonstrated by the approach we took in Table 4, we are ready to suggest what is—all things considered—a more suitable policy for the hypothetical client we have imagined.

Although there was nothing wrong with the policy depicted in Table 4, in the real world we would be more comfortable with a policy that wasn't so "tight." The modified policy that we present below, in Table 5, is much more robust, as we will see; it has a much larger cushion, in case the expected windfall is smaller than anticipated, for example.

"But wait a second," you may object. "I thought the business owner told us upfront that he didn't have any spare cashflow? Of course he would have funded a bigger policy if he could have afforded it, but wasn't the whole *point* that he had nothing to spare?!"

Ah, here is why we went through the process of first showing Table 4. In our experience, once the business owner sees how fast the (gross) cash value and death benefit jump by first flowing the regular tax payments through a policy, he immediately has a change of perspective. He is willing to listen as we explain that he has a much larger cashflow at his disposal.

Specifically, in the case of this particular hypothetical owner, we can say, "We've already seen the possibilities of setting up an IBC policy using your earmarked tax payment as a way of 'bulking up' the policy in the early years, until you make your sale down the road and have extra income that you'll use to knock down the policy loan. But why stop there? If you have a tax liability of $100,000, that means your gross business *profit* was something like $285,000 (if we assume an effective tax rate of 35 percent). *That* is how much you are drawing as profit from your business, on which you owe $100,000 in income tax. So what if we put *the whole gross income* into the policy each year, and then take out the policy loan to make the tax payment (as before)?"

At this point, the business owner is excited to see the illustration, because he realizes the policy will be even more impressive than before.

Table 5. Whole Life Insurance Policy Illustration for 45-year-old, circa 2018

Age	Premium	Loan Amount (during year)	Cumulative Loan Balance (includes interest)	Net Premium Outlay	Annual Dividend (rolled back into policy)	Net Cash Value (accounts for loan balance)	Net Death Benefit (accounts for loan balance)
46	$285k	$0	$0	$285,000	$13,000	$181k	$7.7m
47	$285k	$100k	$105,000	$185,000	$18,000	$330k	$8.2m
48	$285k	$100k	$215,000	$185,000	$23,000	$487k	$8.7m
49	$285k	$100k	$331,000	$185,000	$27,000	$652k	$9.1m
50	$285k	$100k	$453,000	$185,000	$32,000	$825k	$9.6m
51	$285k	$100k	$580,000	$185,000	$34,000	$1.0m	$10.0m
52	$285k	$100k	$714,000	$185,000	$42,000	$1.2m	$10.4m
53	$285k	$100k	$855,000	$185,000	$50,000	$1.4m	$10.8m
54	$285k	$100k	$1.0m	$185,000	$58,000	$1.6m	$11.2m
55	$285k	$100k	$1.2m	$185,000	$65,000	$1.8m	$11.6m
56	$0	$0	$1.2m	$0	$33,000	$1.9m	$6.1m
57	$0	$0	$1.3m	$0	$36,000	$2.0m	$6.1m
58	$0	$0	$1.3m	$0	$38,000	$2.0m	$6.2m
59	$0	$0	$1.4m	$0	$40,000	$2.1m	$6.2m
60	$0	$0	$1.5m	$0	$42,000	$2.2m	$6.2m
...	...	...	...	...	...	...	...
75	$0	$0	$3.1m	$0	$97,000	$3.5m	$6.4m
76	$0	$0	$3.2m	$0	$102,000	$3.6m	$6.4m
77	$0	$0	$3.4m	$0	$107,000	$3.7m	$6.4m

Discussion of Table 5

Now that you, the reader, are more familiar with interpreting policy illustrations, we need only comment on some of the new features in Table 5. The main difference between the previous illustration (in Table 4) and the new one, is that our hypothetical business owner is putting in a gross total premium of $285,000 now, compared to $120,000 before. To repeat, this is the business owner's entire gross profit drawn out of the business for the year, on which he owes $100,000 in income tax. As before, here too in Table 5 we don't have our policy owner borrowing in the first year, because we think it's clearer this way to show the reader exactly what is happening inside the policy. (To repeat, the business owner has the *ability* to borrow in the first year, and if he *were* to do so, then the figures shown in the cash and death benefit columns in Table 5 would be lower in subsequent years.) But starting in Year 2 of the policy, we show the business owner taking $100,000 annual policy loans in order to make the tax payment.

Naturally, by plowing in larger premium payments in the early years, the policy shown in Table 5 grows much more rapidly than the one shown in Table 4. For example, by the fifth year of the policy—when our hypothetical business owner is Age 50—the *net* cash value (i.e. even after accounting for the outstanding policy loan balance) available in Table 5 is $825,000, whereas in Table 4 it was only $147,000. Similarly, the *net* death benefit (even after the policy loan is paid off) available now at Age 50 is $9.6 million, compared to only $3.3 million with the smaller policy from before.

To fill in some of the details of the particular policy design shown in Table 5: There is a base policy carrying an annual premium of $107,000, which has an initial face death benefit coverage of some $3.8 million. That base policy is supplemented by a 10-year term rider with a premium of $6,700 that carries $3.3 million in additional death benefit coverage (for the limited term). Finally, there is a "level paid-up additions" rider, which allows an additional $171,000 of annual premium. Note that all three components add up (with rounding) to the total $285,000 in gross premium that the business owner pays into the policy, during each of the first ten years. We can also deduce from Table 5 that the first year's paid-up additions component (together with the additional life insurance purchased by the dividend being rolled back into the policy) raised the death

Putting IBC Into Action

benefit some $600,000. (This is because the base policy's death benefit is $3.8 million while the term rider gives $3.3 million, for a combined $7.1 million in coverage, yet the right column in Table 5 in the first year shows a total of $7.7 million in total coverage.)

Besides the increase in premium levels, the one major difference in policy design going from Table 4 to Table 5, is that in the latter we have shown the business owner stops making out-of-pocket payments after the tenth year (i.e. at Age 55). The way we actually achieved this was to have the business owner (in the hypothetical world of the illustration) tell the life insurance company at that time to "close up" the policy, so that the next year it is a fully-paid up policy, not requiring further contractual premium payments. This decision caused the (net) death benefit to drop from $11.6 million at the end of the tenth year (Age 55), down to $6.1 million at the end of the eleventh year (Age 56).[iii] In the interest of brevity, we cannot dwell on the intricacies of policy design here; we merely wanted to show the reader yet another possibility when it comes to the construction of a Whole Life policy intended for IBC.

As in our earlier discussion when we analyzed Table 4, here too we haven't explicitly shown the influx of additional income ("windfall") in Table 5. Also, we have only shown the business owner explicitly taking policy loans for the $100,000 annual tax payments, even though he presumably would need to borrow additional amounts since he is putting his entire gross profit into the policy. We haven't shown additional borrowing because it would be arbitrary, and would make it more difficult to contrast the results in Table 5 with those of Table 4. (Also, we note that the business owner who originally "had no spare cashflow" was probably diverting much of his after-tax business income into various investments that he now realizes are *not* as attractive as funding his IBC policy.)

Final Thoughts

As we have stated repeatedly, there is no "one right way" to implement IBC. Each case is unique. Some people, for example, might plow modest amounts of premium into their policy (or policies) for several years before taking out their first loan (for a new car purchase, perhaps). Others might pay relatively large premiums upfront—similar to the pattern depicted in our table above—because they are selling off other assets. Some people might want to die with a small outstanding loan balance, to maximize the policy's function of intergenerational wealth transfer. Others might "run the policy dry" by taking out dividends and then policy loans in the later decades, leaving little *net* death benefit available at the end.

For the hypothetical business owner we discussed in this chapter's example, he had specific numbers that made our two policy designs appropriate. Had our business owner *not* expected to receive a large influx of additional income (at some uncertain date) in the first decade, he probably would have done better to be more conservative with the policy design.

Never forget Nelson Nash's injunction to "play honest banker" with yourself. Just because it is *easy* to take out large policy loans and "let them ride," doesn't mean it's *smart* to do so. The large loan balances show in our tables above carry large interest payments (which the illustrations roll into the growing loan balance), which eat up the growing dividend payments that we have shown. *Given* the story that we told about our business owner, the above structure made sense, but in general you must be very careful about letting such a large loan balance develop. (One specific issue is that if you formally *surrender* your Whole Life policy when it has a large outstanding loan balance, there could be tax implications.[iv]) So we want to be very emphatic that *you must have a long-term financial plan* in which your IBC policy or policies provide the cashflow management. You are "allowed" to let your policy loan balances grow, but make sure you are doing so as part of a sensible strategy that you can follow through to completion.

We hope that this discussion has shown the power of IBC to solve the economic problem faced by business owners and households. At the same time, the nuances of optimal policy design underscore the importance of working with someone who has been trained not just in life insurance but *in IBC*. This is why we recommend that anyone reading this book, or consulting our other materials, continue the conversation with graduates of our training program. These Authorized IBC Practitioners are found at:

www.InfiniteBanking.org/Finder

---

[i] It is possible for a business itself to legally own life insurance policies, but in our experience it is usually best for individuals to own Whole Life policies that are intended for IBC purposes. However, the reasons for this preference lie outside the scope of this introductory book.

[ii] As the Net Premium Outlay column indicates, the out-of-pocket contributions were $120,000 in the first year, and $27,000 in the second and third years.

[iii] To avoid confusion, we stress that the policy depicted in Table 5 is *not* a "10-pay," in which, by design, the base policy is configured to have ten annual premium payments after which it is fully funded. If it *were* a 10-pay, then the death benefit wouldn't fall after the tenth year. Rather, in Table 5 we are showing another option available to policy owners, in which you can choose to "close up" a policy by reducing the amount of paid-up insurance it contains, in order to fulfill your contractual premium obligations. If the business owner had decided to keep the policy "open," he could have continued making the base premium payments, in which case the death benefit would not have fallen and (of course) the numbers in subsequent years would have been much bigger.

[iv] Specifically, when you formally *surrender* a policy, the IRS looks at your historical premium payments to determine your "cost basis." Then if your *gross* cash surrender value is higher than this amount, you have a taxable gain on the difference. (This "makes sense" because it shows how much more you took out of the policy than you put in, and since you surrendered the policy before anybody died, in practice it served as an investment vehicle rather than life insurance.) However, in the case of large outstanding policy loans, this procedure can lead to unpleasant surprises, because the policyholder doesn't actually receive the *gross* cash surrender value, only the *net*

amount after the policy loan balance is paid off. This information about the "taxable gain upon surrender" can be obtained on the illustration provided by the life insurance company, but it's important that the individual understands what it means. It also shows why, generally speaking, you would want to keep such a policy in force, rather than formally surrendering it.

Appendices

Appendices

The Nelson Nash Institute

The Nelson Nash Institute (NNI) is named after the founder of the Infinite Banking Concept (IBC), Nelson Nash. Our mission is to educate and inspire individuals to take control of their financial lives by reclaiming the banking function from outsiders.

Our vision is a free society characterized by creative privatized "banking" solutions independent of government intervention. We recognize that true freedom incorporates financial freedom.

We teach the public how to use permanent Whole Life insurance as the cashflow management vehicle for implementing Infinite Banking. Our IBC Practitioner's Program trains financial services professionals—including life insurance agents but also CPAs and attorneys—on how to properly structure Whole Life insurance policies as "banking" polices for their clients.

The Nelson Nash Institute is unique in the educational/insurance/financial marketplace. We provide education on the theory and application of life insurance to both the general public and the financial services professional, but we are not directly affiliated with the insurance industry.

For more information about the Nelson Nash Institute, go to:

www.InfiniteBanking.org

The IBC Practitioner's Program
(for Financial Professionals)

The IBC Practitioner's Program is an educational program *designed for financial professionals* who wish to make the Infinite Banking Concept (IBC) part of their client relationships. The IBC Practitioner's Program consists of online educational videos (from instructors R. Nelson Nash, L. Carlos Lara, and Robert P. Murphy), a printed Program Manual, and an Exam. Graduates of the program can be sure that they will possess a solid foundation in the theory and implementation of IBC, as well as an understanding of Austrian economics and its unique insights into our monetary and banking institutions.

To ensure the highest degree of professionalism—and that the people entering the program are doing so for the right reasons—applicants must first go through an interview process with the administrators. Furthermore, even after an applicant has completed the formal educational component and passed the final Exam, those new to the industry or to the design of Whole Life policies may be assigned an additional training component of working with an established mentor who is also an Authorized IBC Practitioner.

The overarching purpose of the IBC Practitioner's Program is to provide a growing body of financial professionals who can assist the general public in seceding from the current monetary and banking system. By selecting and training the proper financial professionals to join the ranks of Authorized IBC Practitioners, we can "Build the 10%" and change public opinion.

For more information on the IBC Practitioner's Program, go to:

www.InfiniteBanking.org/practitioners-program/

How to Find an Authorized IBC Practitioner

The information in this book has been designed to make you, the reader, eager to learn more about applying the Infinite Banking Concept (IBC) to your own business or household. This process eventually entails the design of a properly structured, dividend-paying Whole Life policy to suit your particular situation.

As the discussion in this book has amply demonstrated, there are nuances involved in calibrating a Whole Life policy that is intended to serve the purposes of IBC. There are both theoretical and practical considerations in policy design that an outsider—even a professional insurance agent who has read Nelson Nash's books—will simply not know. (Even worse, these outsiders won't *know* they don't know.)

The authors of this book do not sell life insurance to the general public. Instead, we strongly encourage readers interested in applying IBC to their own personal circumstances to find a graduate of the IBC Practitioner's Program. These graduates are listed by state at the following:

www.InfiniteBanking.org/Finder

Furthermore, for best results, we recommend that *before* you contact a practitioner, you first listen to episodes #17 and #18 of the Lara-Murphy Show, available at:

https://lara-murphy.com/podcast/episode-17-guide-starting-ibc-part-1/

and

https://lara-murphy.com/podcast/episode-18-guide-starting-ibc-part-2/

132

About the Authors

L. Carlos Lara is a businessman and owner of several for-profit enterprises. He is also the CEO of United Services and Trust Corporation, a business management consulting firm incorporated in 1976 and headquartered in Nashville, Tennessee. The firm's primary services are capital formation, corporate trusts, debtor-creditor relations, and business crisis counseling.

Lara's background in informal business reorganizations and credit restructuring makes him a regular speaker at business credit conferences. During the 1980s he taught classes in credit management to credit executives seeking the ABCE accreditation, now the Certified Credit Executive (C.C.E.), for the National Association of Credit Management (NACM).

Prior to 2005, Lara held all the required licenses as a Registered Broker-Dealer and Member of the National Association of Securities Dealers (NASD) with extensive experience in the financial services industry.

He is a free-market advocate in the *Austrian School* tradition, frequently writing and speaking on the subject. In 2010 he co-authored with economist Robert P. Murphy, *How Privatized Banking **Really** Works: Integrating Austrian Economics With The Infinite Banking Concept.* Also with Robert Murphy, he is editor of the *Lara-Murphy Report*, an online publication specializing in financial markets, *Austrian* economics and Nelson Nash's *Infinite Banking Concept (IBC)*.

In 2013 he co-produced with Nelson Nash, Robert P. Murphy, and David Stearns, the *IBC Practitioner Program*, an educational training course on the theory of the *Infinite Banking Concept (IBC)*, which is designed for licensed financial professionals.

For additional information and useful reference material about Carlos Lara, including additional reading lists, videos, podcasts and other available resources visit: *https://lara-murphy.com*.

Robert P. Murphy is Research Assistant Professor with the Free Market Institute at Texas Tech University. He has a PhD in economics from New York University. He is also a Senior Fellow with the Mises Institute, Chief Economist for the Institute for Energy Research, Senior Fellow for the Fraser Institute, and a Research Fellow with the Independent Institute.

Murphy is the author of hundreds of articles and many books explaining economics to the layperson. These include *The Politically Incorrect Guide to Capitalism* (Regnery 2007), *The Politically Incorrect Guide to the Great Depression and the New Deal* (Regnery 2009), the Study Guide (Mises Institute 2006) to Murray Rothbard's *Man, Economy, and State*, the textbook *Lessons for the Young Economist* (Mises Institute 2010), the Study Guide (Mises Institute 2011) to Ludwig von Mises' *The Theory of Money and Credit*, and—with ER doctor Doug McGuff—a book on the economics of U.S. health care and insurance, *The Primal Prescription* (Primal Nutrition 2015). In addition, Murphy's book *Choice: Cooperation, Enterprise, and Human Action* (Independent Institute 2015) offers a comprehensive introduction to, and exposition of, the work of Austrian School economist Ludwig von Mises.

Murphy's two main academic research areas are monetary/interest theory, and the economics of climate change. He has testified before Congress several times on these topics. His academic publications include "Dangers of the One-Good Model: Böhm-Bawerk's Critique of the 'Naïve Productivity Theory' of Interest," *Journal of the History of Economic Thought*, Vol. 27, Issue 4, Dec. 2005; and (with climate scientists Patrick Michaels and Paul Knappenberger) "The Case Against a U.S. Carbon Tax," *Cato Institute* Policy Analysis No. 801, Oct. 2016.

Murphy is co-creator of the Infinite Banking Concept (IBC) Practitioner's Program for Financial Professionals, and (with Carlos Lara) produces the monthly financial publication *The Lara-Murphy Report*. He is also co-author (with Carlos Lara) of the 2010 book, *How Privatized Banking **Really** Works*, which integrates Austrian economics with the Infinite Banking Concept. Their joint website is www.Lara-Murphy.com.

Along with Tom Woods, Murphy is also co-host of the popular podcast "Contra Krugman." His personal website is www.ConsultingByRPM.com.

Nelson Nash is the discoverer of The Infinite Banking Concept™ and the author of *Becoming Your Own Banker©* and *Building Your Warehouse of Wealth©*.

A native of Georgia, Nelson received his BS degree in Forestry from the University of Georgia in 1952. He worked as a forestry consultant for 10 years in North Carolina where he introduced several innovative practices to private forestry. He was also active in real estate investing for over 30 years.

He spent over 35 years as an agent for The Equitable Life Assurance Society of the U.S. and with The Guardian. He is a life member of the Million Dollar Roundtable (MDRT) and a member of Equitable Life Assurance Society's Hall of Fame. He a Chartered Life Underwriter (CLU).

A pilot for 60 years, Nash flew with the Army National Guard, and earned Master Aviator Wings during his 30 years of military service. He has spent over 60 years in the study of economics (The Austrian School of thought). This began with The Foundation for Economic Education (FEE). He is a charter member of the Leonard E. Read Society.

He has been married to Mary W. Nash for more than 65 years. The couple live in Birmingham, Alabama and have three children, ten grandchildren and seven great-grandchildren.

David Stearns joined Infinite Banking Concepts in June 2004 after retiring from the U.S. Army as a Lieutenant Colonel.

David served 27 years in the Army, first as a field artillery officer, then as an Army aviator. As with all military officers, he served in a variety of assignments including unit command, operations, safety, and systems analysis/operations research. David served throughout the Continental U.S. and world-wide with a long tour in Egypt and multiple deployments to Germany, Korea, and Kuwait.

David is the President of Infinite Banking Concepts LLC and a Director of the Nelson Nash Institute.

David graduated with a BA degree from Buffalo State College in 1975, and received a Masters of Public Administration from Auburn University, Montgomery in 1992.

He has been married to Kimberly Stearns since 1979. They live in Birmingham, Alabama and have four children and six grandchildren.